Partners in Learning

Students, Teachers, and the School Library

Ray Doiron
and
Judy Davies

Foreword by
Ken Haycock

1998
Libraries Unlimited, Inc.
and Its Division
Teacher Ideas Press
Englewood, Colorado

Libraries Unlimited, Inc.
and Its Division
Teacher Ideas Press
P.O. Box 6633
Englewood, CO 80155-6633
www.lu.com

Production Editor: Stephen Haenel
Copy Editor: Susan Brown
Proofreader: Matthew Stewart
Indexer: Kay Meredith Dusheck
Layout and Design: Michael Florman

Library of Congress Cataloging-in-Publication Data

Doiron, Ray.
    Partners in learning : students, teachers, and the school library
/ Ray Doiron and Judy Davies ; foreword by Ken Haycock.
    xiii, 182 p. 22x28 cm.
    Includes bibliographical references (p. 171) and index.
    ISBN 1-56308-552-6
    1. Elementary school libraries--Activity programs--United States.
2. Elementary school libraries--Activity programs--Canada.
3. Library orientation for school children--United States.
4. Library orientation for school children--Canada. 5. Elementary
school teaching--United States. 6. Elementary school teaching--
Canada. 7. Teaching teams--United States. 8. Teaching teams--
Canada. I. Davies, Judy, 1947-   . II. Title.
Z675.S3D585 1997
027.8'222--dc21   97-30591
                                                                    CIP

Dedication

A collaboration between two colleagues always involves bringing together a vast number of teaching experiences that both have shared with dozens of their previous colleagues. This was especially true in this endeavor. We worked in Glen Stewart Elementary School and L.M. Montgomery Elementary School for more than sixteen years, and during that time we worked with some of the best elementary classroom teachers in our part of the world. They were willing to try new ideas, to work collaboratively with their peers, and to provide their students with the best learning experiences possible. We dedicate this book to them and hope we have captured their spirit, commitment, expertise, and joy in teaching elementary students.

Table of Contents

Foreword

Students in schools with well-equipped library resource centers and professional teacher-librarians perform better on outcome measures of literacy, information handling and use, and mastery of subject content. This result is possible, however, only when there is recognition that the library program is a partnership—a partnership of the teacher-librarian and the classroom teacher, supported by school district leadership.

The principal is the key player in the development of well-integrated, flexible programs and demonstrates specific supportive behaviors in developing teacher awareness and commitment to cooperative program planning and teaching with the teacher-librarian. Similarly, the teacher-librarian's leadership abilities, including the capacity to connect collaboration to the principal's agenda, affect the implementation of this complex innovation.

An essential first step to improvement of library programs is clarification of the role of the teacher-librarian. Inasmuch as the program's effectiveness, in terms of student achievement, rests on planning between the classroom teacher and the teacher-librarian, it is essential that the primary task of the teacher-librarian involves initiation of the planning and team-teaching partnership. Professional collaboration and joint implementation of resource-based units of study, in flexibly scheduled resource centers, are critical to improved student learning.

The classroom teacher brings to the planning partnership knowledge of curriculum, of the classroom program, and of student needs and abilities. The teacher-librarian brings to the planning partnership knowledge of curriculum, of the resources to support student learning in the program, and of the skills and strategies necessary for students to handle information and ideas effectively. When these areas of expertise are integrated, the result is teaching and learning with information skills and strategies incorporated in resource-based instruction in thoughtful and relevant ways. Student learning is assessed jointly through careful monitoring and authentic products.

Study after study tells us that teachers with experience in this cooperative program planning and teaching with the teacher-librarian have a more positive view of the role of the teacher-librarian and welcome closer collaboration.

Ray Doiron and Judy Davies represent the best of partnerships and the best of teacher-librarianship. They are educated and experienced as both classroom teachers and teacher-librarians—they are front-line people. They are consummate professionals, reflecting on their practice and deriving meaning from their work through linkages with the school and implementation of guiding principles for effectiveness. They have gathered innumerable ideas and given voice to the successful experiences of teachers and students. They provide many examples to demonstrate the planning and teaching partnership of the classroom teacher and teacher-librarian.

What is clear is the contribution of the authors to the quality of experiences of students and teachers in their schools. Here are two professionals, working with very different school staffs and with very limited resources, coming together to find common ground and provide examples that can be implemented elsewhere with equal effect.

Working through a firm research base, proven methods, and practical examples, the authors provide the reader with a solid philosophy for an exemplary program and the models necessary to carry it forward. If mirror images of the collaborative work exemplified in this book appeared in other schools throughout the continent, we would have no difficulty graduating concerned, considerate, and literate students committed to informed decision making and lifelong learning, a worthy goal indeed.

—Ken Haycock

Acknowledgments

The impetus for this book grew out of a very intense and rewarding time in our teaching careers. Our goals were to reflect on those sixteen years and give voice to the teaching and learning experiences we had. Those experiences did not happen in isolation, and for their professional help throughout our time in the role of teacher-librarian, we wish to acknowledge the following people:

To the teacher-librarian community in our home province of Prince Edward Island, who have supported us and inspired us during our careers as teacher-librarians.

To the classroom teachers at L.M. Montgomery Elementary School and Glen Stewart Elementary School, who worked with us as we explored the potential of an integrated school library program.

To the administrators of our schools, George Doughart, Carol MacMillan, and Maitland MacIsaac, who entered into a true collaboration with us as we charted a new direction for the school library resource centers in our schools.

To our colleagues across Canada who provided us with a national perspective on the trends and issues facing school librarianship, especially to Dr. Ken Haycock for agreeing to add a foreword to the book. Ken's foundational work on the role of the teacher-librarian inspired us to embrace the vision of an integrated school library program.

On a personal note, Ray would like to acknowledge his wife Elizabeth and his three children, who make his family collaboration such a rewarding experience and who always support his professional and personal goals.

Judy wishes to thank her husband, Richard, and the "flock" at Millery Farm, especially Bradley and Elisa, for their endless encouragement, support, and patience throughout this and many other projects.

In the preparation of the manuscript, many thanks to our colleagues who shared their ideas and let us photograph them at work in their school libraries. The Prince Edward Island schools and their teacher-librarians used throughout the book are Elizabeth Greenan, Amherst Cove School; Helen McQuaid, Parkside Elementary School; and Pauline Walker, Queen Elizabeth Elementary School. Special thanks to Andrea Demers for her work preparing the graphics for the book.

CHAPTER ONE

PARTNERS IN THE SCHOOL LIBRARY PROGRAM

In the opening chapter we examine the current context for school library resource center programs. Some historical perspective is given and then a discussion follows of some of the factors that have forced educators to reposition the school library as a focal point of contemporary literacy programs. It calls for a strengthening of the partnership between classroom teachers and teacher-librarians to provide students with purposeful and integrated learning experiences.

A New Vision of the School Library Resource Center Program

School libraries have changed. Once quiet corners where books were collected for supplementary reading purposes, libraries have expanded and grown to meet the needs of a constantly evolving educational system where an abundance of quality resources are essential. The traditional role of warehousing resources and lending them out to teachers and students is still an important aspect, but this is certainly not the only reason for having a school library resource (media) center (SLRC).

Activities that occur within this facility have also evolved beyond the circulation and management of materials to include a vast assortment of learning opportunities for individuals and groups. While the teacher-librarian has retained some aspects of the traditional role, which emphasized the technical and clerical duties of librarianship, the role has evolved to include a more integrated approach to the teaching of the skills necessary for finding, accessing, evaluating, using, and sharing information.

Several factors affected the evolution of the present-day SLRC. The first was the enormous increase in the number of resource-based programs that demand larger and richer resources for their full implementation. Coupled with this was the development of a variety of exciting new teaching strategies that respond to significant changes in educational theory and practice related to our understanding of how learning takes place and that focus on creating a child-centered, active learning environment. Third, the pervasive influence of various information technologies, such as Online Public Access Catalogs (OPAC), CD-ROM, the World Wide Web, and automated circulation systems have radically altered the way we conceive of a library and how it should operate. The school library resource center plays a central role in a school's overall plan for information literacy. This places the school library program within the context of the information age, where it reflects the same enormous increase in knowledge, technology, and general societal change that has shaped the entire educational system.

The Information Age

The modern SLRC is not confined to an isolated corner within the school. Its collections of resources and the programs it offers extend well beyond the physical facility. The community, and indeed the world, are accessible to the individual school library program through the use of fax machines, modems, communication satellites, the Internet, and networked services. Students are learning to use exciting new computer technology that makes the card catalog obsolete. Now the personal computer makes searching for information easier and allows students more time to actually use the information they locate.

Teacher-librarians, realizing the importance of teaching information-processing skills when there is a real purpose, are responding with appropriate instruction in the use of these new technological tools. As their students explore databases, such as those stored on CD-ROM format (where an entire encyclopedia may be available on a single disc), teacher-librarians are assuming a new set of information-related responsibilities. These responsibilities are based on the assumption that learning how to learn combined with critical-thinking skills and the ability to reflect on one's learning are the most important things students need to know for their future in the information age. Together these educational principles imply a new vision for how a school library resource center functions, a vision grounded in the concept of information literacy.

Changes in Education

Several significant changes in education have had an impact on the school library program:

1. A more balanced emphasis on process and product has become increasingly important. Educators focus more on developing concepts and skills than simply mastering a specified content.

2. Tied to this influence is the fact that subject area teachers recognize that the content of their courses is too vast and changes too quickly to be ever mastered with one textbook.

3. Instruction and learning are far more holistic and student-centered, with increased opportunities for the integration of information-processing, critical-thinking, and problem-solving skills.

4. Collaborative learning has become much more common in our classrooms in response to demands that the future workplace will require teamwork and problem solvers. This creates new demands for using a wide range of resources in more flexible facilities for more purposeful activities.

5. Technology is no longer an "extra" added to the educational agenda. It is an integral part of all new curriculum initiatives and a pervasive influence across the system.

When combined, these forces are resulting in the necessary redefinition of the traditional roles of the classroom teacher, the teacher-librarian, and the student as they seek to determine common educational goals. A new type of school library program emerges from these factors that is forcing a greater cooperation and shared commitment to the provision of a more meaningful and rich teaching/learning environment.

Key Components of the School Library Resource Center Program

Several concepts are consistently mentioned when discussing the new vision of the school library resource center program. These are dealt with in more detail in subsequent chapters, but they need some clarification here before the partnership among the teacher-librarian, the classroom teacher, and students can be clearly articulated. The traditional who, what, where, when, why, and how questions will help organize the description of these key concepts.

What Is the School Library Resource Center Program?

The Canadian School Library Association defines the school library resource center program as one that is an integral part of the instructional program of the school and happens when information skills are integrated in a developmental and sequential way with subject-specific skills and content. Through such planned and purposeful activities students learn how to retrieve, evaluate, organize, share and apply information objectively, critically, and independently. As well, they are given opportunities to grow intellectually, aesthetically, and personally (CSLA, 1988).

In the United States, the *Information Power* (American Association of School Libraries, 1988) document states that the school library media program "that is fully integrated into the school's curriculum is central to the learning process. It is critical in students' intellectual development, promoting the love of learning and conveying the importance of using and evaluating information and ideas throughout life" (p. 15).

Who Gets Involved in the School Library Resource Center Program?

The development of the school library resource center is led by a teacher-librarian, who is recognized as "an outstanding or master teacher with specialized advanced education in the selection, organization, management and use of learning resources and the school library resource center" (Haycock, 1990). The teacher-librarian works in partnership with classroom teachers and students to develop resource-based units of study (RBUs) that teach information skills, nurture an appreciation for literature and the aesthetic qualities of life, as well as develop strategies that recognize learning as a lifelong process.

Where Does the School Library Resource Center Program Operate?

This program is incorporated throughout the school environment. Many activities will happen in a well-stocked and flexibly organized school library resource center, but also the teacher-librarian will work directly in classrooms, and classroom teachers and students will use the school library resource center as an extension of the classroom learning environment.

When Does This Program Operate?

There are no prescribed times to teach information skills or to borrow materials. Information skills pervade the curriculum and are learned best when integrated with purposeful activities that give students a sense of ownership and control over their learning. School library programs operate on a flexible timetable that allows classroom teachers access to the teaching skills of the teacher-librarian when they want to collaborate for developing specific information skills. Students and teachers have an open, flexible time to browse and borrow resources from the school library resource center.

Why Bother Developing a School Library Resource Center Program?

The concept of the school library resource center is an essential element in all school districts if we are to achieve learning outcomes that prepare students for life in an information world. The effort to redefine and redesign school library programs is an attempt to ensure the most effective use of resources and to enable all educators to make learning a more active and meaningful experience for the teacher and the learner.

How Do School Library Resource Center Programs Operate?

To achieve the goals of an integrated school library resource center program, a collaborative planning and teaching process must be activated. This collaborative process develops in a supportive school environment, has an agreed upon set of goals and procedures that assign roles to each of the partners, and ensures that an overall schoolwide plan for information skills is developed and implemented.

Clarifying the New Partnership

The new vision for the school library resource center is grounded in the partnership among the classroom teacher, the teacher-librarian, and the student, as well as the integration of resources and information-processing skills into the school curriculum. This makes the school library an integral part of the total school program. It is referred to as the hub of the school, the center for resource collections within the school, and the point of access for resources and information within the community or within a network of schools.

However, the school library program does not operate as a separate curricular area with an isolated set of "library skills" taught in a prescribed way by the librarian. Instead, it supports the entire school curriculum with a wide range of appropriate resources and with opportunities to make the best possible use of those resources by integrating the teaching of information skills with the instructional goals of the classroom. This model of "resource-based" learning provides opportunities to develop learning activities in all subject areas that are carefully planned, taught, and evaluated by the classroom teachers, teacher-librarians, and their students, working through a more collaborative learning process. Together, they are responding to the pressures of the information age and movements for educational change to design and implement curriculum that is relevant, purposeful, and student centered.

By using the best possible resources for the integration of information skills and critical-thinking skills with curriculum concepts and content, this new partnership is achieving results that are both satisfying and exciting for everyone involved.

Although the classroom teacher, the teacher-librarian, and the student are the key players in this scenario, the school administrator and the district area curriculum specialist also play critical roles by supporting the efforts of these teaching partners and by creating an environment where this professional collaboration is allowed to flourish. This takes the form of providing curriculum leadership, supplying adequate budgets, establishing timetables that encourage the collaborative process, and actively monitoring the planning, implementation, and evaluation components of the program.

Figure 1.1 provides a model of the partnership inherent in a school library resource center program by listing specific areas of expertise for each of the key players and situating them within the context of strong administrative support and leadership. Each role is examined more closely in the following sections.

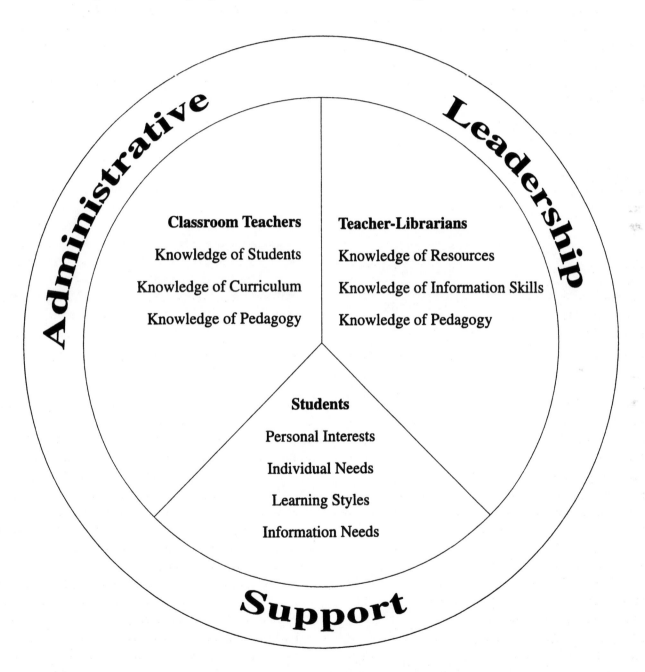

Fig. 1.1. A Partnership for Developing Integrated School Library Resource Center Programs.

The Role of the Classroom Teacher

Area of Expertise

Throughout the past decade classroom teachers have been inundated with many new trends in education that are placing a tremendous pressure on them to include more and more in their programs. They know they can't cover all the content that is needed. They know they must concentrate on the processes involved in learning and not look just at the learner's product. They know they must integrate learning to help students see the links that exist across the curriculum. Evaluation rests in a more holistic look at the progress made over a period of time. Teachers must make choices in the types of experiences they will provide to help build a positive and productive learning environment for their students.

Two areas continue to be the strengths that classroom teachers bring to the curriculum-planning process. Classroom teachers know their students— their strengths and weaknesses, attitudes, and interests. They assess their needs and provide learning experiences that will help address those needs. In addition, classroom teachers know their own programs. They know the content they want to cover, the thinking skills and strategies they want to develop, and the cognitive processes they want to use to develop learning. They are curriculum developers who increasingly recognize the need to include many different resources in the teaching/learning situation. These two areas become the major components of the classroom teacher's role in the partnership with the teacher-librarian.

Curriculum Development

Classroom teachers have incorporated many of the new theories of how learning takes place into their curriculum plans. They are no longer guided by a single text in developing their programs, but rather they pull in a variety of resources and decide what is relevant to the concepts, processes, and content they wish to develop. This involves planning and evaluation that is long range as well as responsive to students' personal interests and experiences.

Classroom teachers recognize that skills are learned better when they are taught in meaningful contexts rather than in isolation. They also know that many of the same skills and strategies developed in their grade/subject curriculum are used when students use any resource material. These are the same factors that have moved the teacher-librarian away from teaching information skills in isolation. It should also be noted that the skills and strategies applied to information processing are the same for students working in the classroom or in the school library. This common ground and perspective forges a natural link between the classroom teacher and the teacher-librarian in the development of the school curriculum.

Classroom teachers naturally develop a personal repertoire of teaching strategies that work in different learning situations. They are also encouraged to use a variety of teaching strategies in their programs to respond to student interests and various learning styles. The resource-based learning model advocated by the school library program becomes another strategy that classroom teachers add to their repertoire. Several times during the school year they call on the teacher-librarian to activate a partnership that allows both to share in the planning, preparing, teaching, and evaluating of units of study that reflect the learning needs and interests of their students. This helps to reduce the student-teacher ratio during the completion of teaching/learning activities. It also combines the expertise of two teachers who work together to provide meaningful learning experiences for students.

Using Resources

In today's classrooms, there are many more teaching/learning materials being used in the daily activities of students and teachers than ever before. Both demand to have the best quality and a large quantity of resources. For most subject areas, learners use books, magazines, audio visual materials, computer software, guest speakers, and various human and community resources. Classroom teachers cannot be expected to know all the available resources and when and how to use them. This need provides another natural link between the classroom and the school library.

Planning for the use of resources then, becomes a vital factor in curriculum development. The teacher-librarian builds a strong centralized resource that reflects the curriculum needs of the school, ensuring that all staff and students have access to the materials when they are needed. Classroom teachers are able to access the centralized collection and decide how best to use the materials. Bringing this about involves planning. The resources may be set up at learning stations in the library or in the classroom; they may be located in an information station designed to reserve and display all the available materials on a certain subject; they could be signed out by the classroom teacher for use in their daily work.

With the heavy emphasis on literature-based programs, many classroom teachers like to build small classroom libraries that house some of their favorite titles or frequently used titles. However, with the cost of resources and limited (even shrinking) budgets, the centralizing of resources seems to make more sense since it allows for the sharing of many more resources over the long term.

The Role of the Teacher-Librarian

Area of Expertise

With the changes in the function of the school library have come the redefining of the role of the person working in the school library. Effective teacher-librarians combine their knowledge of resources with their knowledge of information skills to develop sound pedagogical strategies that nurture a love for literature, build aesthetic and creative experiences, develop critical thinking, and produce effective users of information. The people responsible for the school library were traditionally referred to as school librarians. Sometimes they had special training in school librarianship or they were classroom teachers asked to take on the role. They were good organizers and managers, who provided resources for students and teachers and taught a set of skills specific to using a library. The emerging role of the school library resource center as a more integrated part of the school curriculum has changed the school librarian into a *teacher-librarian,* giving more emphasis to the teaching component of the role. As well, their responsibility for collection management and development has been broadened to include information technology and to make the development of resources a more collaborative process between the classroom and the centralized facility.

Teacher-librarians continue to specialize in resources and information skills, but added to that is the responsibility for providing instructional leadership within their school. This places the teacher-librarian at a key point in curriculum development within a school, able to act as an agent for change as schools restructure to include many of the newly emerging educational trends, such as cooperative learning, holistic learning, outcome-based learning, and resource-based learning. The major roles of the teacher-librarian within the school library program are described in more detail below.

Collection Management and Development

With the ever-increasing demand for information comes the need for better and better resources. Teacher-librarians continue to spend a great deal of time selecting, processing, and managing an ever-increasing number of resources. Not only are more resources needed but also varying types are needed, as students and teachers try to meet the challenge of this information age. Books of all kinds continue to be the mainstay of the school library resource center collection, but they are not the only resource needed. Audio-visual materials, periodicals, reference materials, picture and pamphlet files, computer hardware and software, human and community resources, and student- and teacher-made materials are only part of the diverse nature of a school library resource center collection designed to meet the needs of today's teaching/learning environment.

The teacher-librarian acts as an expert in resources, able to suggest and provide suitable resources during the planning, teaching, and evaluating processes that are so critical in the resource-based learning model. Procedures for managing the use of resources also complements this partnership. Some materials may be used in the classroom, some in the school library; some may enrich a topic of study, whereas others form the focal point for students to use in learning activities. Some materials will be used independently, whereas others will be managed in learning stations where groups or individuals complete an activity.

Keeping a handle on the resources and providing accessibility to learning materials is fundamental to the successful operation of the school library. Fortunately many school libraries have become computerized, providing much needed assistance for teacher-librarians in the management and organization of resources. Improved accessibility, better accountability for holdings, and simpler, user-friendly procedures are some of the benefits of automated systems. Teacher-librarians have been able to streamline their management procedures and can offer students and classroom teachers more direct instructional time. The more the teacher-librarian can rely on the management capabilities of computerized library systems to take care of so many of the minute clerical responsibilities, the more time will be available for the professional responsibilities of curriculum development and instructional leadership.

Curriculum Development

In addition to being an expert in resources, the teacher-librarian also knows the school curriculum extremely well. During the planning process, the teacher-librarian brings a thorough understanding of information literacy and its accompanying skills and how they may be integrated into the grade or subject level being discussed. The teacher-librarian helps classroom teachers develop resource-based units of study that broaden their use of resources and incorporate information skills into their programs. Strategies for activating resource-based learning are more easily realized when the teacher-librarian enters fully into the curriculum-planning process.

Rather than directing a parallel program of "library skills" that may coincide periodically with what classroom teachers are doing, teacher-librarians look for opportunities to integrate the use of resources and the skills needed to make the resources both physically and intellectually accessible. They offer their combined expertise in the areas of resources and information literacy so that an overall plan for the development of information processing can be developed in the school. Students and classroom teachers recognize the teacher-librarian as a curriculum person, one who has a lot to offer the teaching/learning environment.

Instructional Leadership

Teacher-librarians are in the unique position of being able to act as instructional leaders in schools because they work with all students and all teachers. They also work closely with the school administration to develop a plan of action for the school library resource center program, which usually involves some form of staff development to bring about the proposed changes. Since that change takes place over time, teacher-librarians often develops skills that facilitate and encourage change. They may help all staff in changing their teaching styles to include more opportunities for resource-based learning, cooperative learning, holistic learning, and student-centered learning.

Many principals recognize how valuable teacher-librarians can be as they pursue their goals for improving instruction. By building a strong relationship, these two people can strengthen the educational environment of the school.

Teacher-librarians include in this role of instructional leadership a strong voice in the advocacy and development of literacy. They have broadened their traditional roles of storytelling and story reading to include programs that deepen students' understanding of the importance of writers and all those associated with the creation of new materials. With a constant awareness of excellence, teacher-librarians purchase and promote all sorts of materials to meet the ever-increasing demands of students and classroom teachers. Their traditional role as specialists in children's literature is now seen as a shared responsibility with classroom teachers, who have included more literature in their programs. Students recognize teacher-librarians as people dedicated to the goals of literacy, and classroom teachers rely heavily on teacher-librarians to provide new and worthwhile titles for their classroom literacy programs.

The Role of the Student

Area of Expertise

In many of the curriculum-planning models developed over the past twenty years, very little mention is made of the role students play in determining what the school curriculum looks like. At the same time, we know that educational movements like student-centered learning, cooperative learning, and active learning encourage educators to have students set goals for themselves and take more ownership of their learning. Just as the teacher-librarian and the classroom teacher bring certain areas of expertise to the planning process, so too do students.

Students are most aware of their own personal interests and individual talents. They are challenging us more and more to recognize these abilities and let them use them to their fullest potential. Students today also are voracious users of media to entertain themselves and to gather information. They are far more visual in their learning styles and much more comfortable with high-tech materials. Too often the school situation fails to take advantage of their natural abilities with multimedia.

Although our students have a great demand for information, they also need critical skills to be able to function effectively in an information-rich society. These two factors exert a great influence on what types of school experiences are most meaningful and useful to them.

The Demand for Information

The world of the young learner is filled with information coming from dozens of different sources. They no longer rely on one or two adults and a few school textbooks for the information they need to live in today's complex society. Living with television, computers, video games, music videos, films, telephones, and other basically visual media have created an enormous demand for information by students. They expect to be given the information freely and to be allowed to have access to whatever information they feel is needed at the time. This situation emphasizes the fact that we need to include information literacy high on the list of what we do at school. If we continue to insist that certain content must be covered to the exclusion of student input, then we run the danger of becoming obsolete in the minds of the learners we serve. They will rely more on sources of information beyond the school and not really have the skills to deal effectively and critically with the huge quantity of information that is available out there.

The Demand for Resources

No other generation of learners has had at their disposal so many useful and exciting materials from which to choose their recreational and informational reading. Book publishers are providing richer and more interesting informational literature all the time. Students read as much, if not more, nonfiction as fiction and at an even earlier age. By the time they get to school, students have experienced films, videos, several music formats, television, electronic toys, computers, and books that seem to provide an endless variety of stimuli. When students start to prepare projects, they know that the ways of sharing information are also varied. They expect that when they gather information for a presentation or to prepare a final product, they will do so in a multimedia format that will include a written or oral component and a variety of visuals that will enhance the final outcome.

The resources available to teachers also reflect the demand for information to be presented in a varied and stimulating way. As they prepare themes or units of study, teachers recognize the need to provide students with several alternative resources from which they can access, retrieve, process, and produce information. Educators understand more about how students learn, and their curriculum planning reflects the need to choose resources that are attuned to visual, auditory, and kinesthetic learning styles.

Information Skills

There are many skills and strategies that make it possible to access, evaluate, and critically use information in all its myriad forms. These skills and strategies help us find, organize, prepare, present, and use information in differing ways and for differing purposes. They were known traditionally as "research" skills, but have come to be called information skills and strategies applied within an overall information process. They, too, are seen as "basic skills" that pervade the curriculum. In mathematics, science, social studies, health, language arts, and the creative and performing arts, learners need and use information. They apply the same basic information skills and strategies in each of the curriculum areas.

The growing demand for information and the added need to provide a wide variety of resources have created an increased awareness of the importance of developing strong information skills and strategies amongst our students. Many of these skills are familiar to us, but traditionally they were taught in isolation from the information needs of the students. Students learned about methods of collecting information, recording information, and organizing information at times predetermined by an out-of-context program. When they had some real need to engage in the information process, very

little transfer of the previous learning took place. With other areas of our educational programs, we have learned that skills are best taught when integrated into opportunities to use them in real situations. The same principle holds true for developing information literacy.

If they are to develop information literacy skills, students need experiences that will enable them to call on the appropriate strategies to process information effectively and efficiently. These skills and strategies must be developed within a cooperative framework that engages teachers and students in problem-solving situations centered on appropriate and accessible resources. Students respond positively to the collaborative nature of this resource-based approach, and classroom teachers and teacher-librarians quickly recognize the strengths of working as partners in the development of the information process.

Benefits of the Partnership

When teacher-librarians, classroom teachers, and students work within a collaborative partnership, they share in a variety of benefits, which include

1. more effective use of resources;

2. more effective use of teaching time;

3. integration of educational technologies;

4. shared efforts at promoting literacy; and

5. developing the goal of lifelong learning.

By focusing on providing many opportunities to activate this partnership, educators will establish a shared responsibility for developing independent, lifelong learners.

Effective Use of Resources

As curriculum and educational programs move away from textbooks, teachers need more resources for instruction and learning. These resources are seldom produced for a single purpose or program and often serve many purposes. So classroom teachers are faced with the enormous task of setting instructional goals and looking for methods and materials that help them teach the content, concepts, skills, and strategies. This task seems less daunting when teachers and teacher-librarians work as partners.

To the classroom teachers will accrue the benefits of using a greater variety of resources to create learning experiences that are more relevant and purposeful. Teacher-librarians are able to integrate the school library resource center goals into the overall school plan for information literacy.

Teacher-librarians spend a great deal of time and effort carefully selecting educational resources that support the curriculum for both instructional and collaborative or independent learning purposes. These resources serve many functions and are produced in a variety of formats. Some may be more appropriate to reinforce a particular aspect of the curriculum, whereas others contain specific content. For example, a filmstrip kit or interactive computer software package may be designed to provide key information suitable for a fifth-grade science program, whereas a video about a well-known author of children's books may contain information useful for a number of learning activities at different grade levels for more than one part of the curriculum.

These resources may come from professional production and publishing companies, but it is becoming more common to include quality resource materials that have been created by educators or community agencies. Formats vary and can be selected for their appropriateness for the teaching/learning activity. Print resources may include books in a variety of bindings as well as big books, pamphlets, magazines, pictures, and study prints.

Nonprint resources may be audio-visual in nature, including audio and video cassettes, videodiscs, films, filmstrips, or slides. Computer resources are available in software packages or CD-ROM materials that serve a variety of functions, such as exciting electronic reference materials. There may also be useful collections of artifacts and manipulatives or other materials for hands-on activities.

Some school library resource centers have large collections of nonprint materials on site, in addition to their print collections. Sometimes these nonprint resources are located elsewhere in centralized district collections. This districtwide sharing is one efficient and cost-saving approach, since more expensive materials that are used less frequently can still be available to students and teachers. Within the school as well, a centralized resource collection is preferred over small classroom or grade- or subject-area collections. Centralization is cost effective, allows for better management of resources, and helps ensure resources are effectively used within the curriculum. Resources that were purchased by a school should be available for all to use, even though they appear appropriate for one grade level or one particular program. A teacher-librarian can coordinate and manage these resources so that those who need them most can get them, and those who may have alternate or supplementary reasons for wanting the resources can still access them.

Where the storage and circulation of learning resources is not carefully managed, there will inevitably be problems. The teacher-librarian's expertise in managing as well as selecting resources ensures that the school library resource center's collection is accessible to the teachers and students who use it. As always, teacher-librarians are continually improving methods for organizing, storing, and circulating resources when they are in use or available for use. The card catalog or the computerized OPAC contains the necessary information to locate these items by their titles, authors, or subject headings. Learning centers may be located in the school library resource center or in classrooms, where the selected resources are placed for student activities and for others to browse and view. These are most successful when teachers and teacher-librarians and their students work together to match their teaching and learning goals with appropriate resources.

Frequently the resources that support a particular curriculum theme are gathered together and made available for use in one or more classroom settings. These resources may include a variety of print and nonprint materials that have been selected because they contain important content, concepts, and presentation that are suitable for students within a grade level or subject area. Many teacher-librarians and classroom teachers have collaborated to organize thematic collections of resources. These are often placed in "theme boxes" or plastic containers that are easily transported to any location in the school. Some school districts use theme boxes to supplement resources when similar themes are taught in many schools. They are then readily available whenever these recurring themes or topics are planned and taught.

Although the "theme box" method is a practical, time-saving approach to one aspect of resource management, teacher-librarians must also make materials available to students and teachers on an individual basis. The use of resource lists or computer-generated bibliographies enable the teacher-librarian to quickly gather the resources needed for independent inquiry or as supplementary materials for a theme. These resources may then remain in circulation until requested for some planned instructional purpose.

Resource collecting extends well beyond the school library resource center into other library collections or community collections. Teacher-librarians are able to access resources through interlibrary loan arrangements with other school or public libraries, and they often have information about government or private agencies or individuals who are willing to share relevant information that can enrich the school's curriculum.

Effective Use of Teaching Time

When teachers and teacher-librarians work together to provide opportunities for using resources to improve teaching and learning, they discover the educational benefits resulting from collaborative planning and teaching. An obvious benefit is the addition of another teacher (i.e., the teacher-librarian) to the instructional team. Students have another professional to facilitate their learning; teachers have another colleague with whom they can share the tasks of planning, teaching, and evaluating the learning process.

School-based curriculum planning includes the development of major skills, strategies, and processes, as well as relevant content and concepts. Curriculum development is often holistic and child-centered, with an emphasis on meaningful activities organized around a central theme. This type of curriculum cannot be developed by an individual teacher working in isolation. With classroom teachers and teacher-librarians working together, the curriculum development process is streamlined and the result is a more integrated and consistent set of curriculum outcomes.

The information process, like the other educational processes, is not effectively developed in isolation, nor is it the sole responsibility of one educator or one grade level within the system. When the school's professional team decides to include the information process in their curriculum planning, they will identify skills and strategies that are important at each developmental level. Planned opportunities to engage students in the purposeful practice of each of the stages will be included within the process, and the development of the information process will be seen as pervasive to all grade levels and all areas across the curriculum.

The development of a school-based plan for information skills, taught within the framework of the information process, will ensure a consistent development of the skills and strategies students need to retrieve, access, process, and share information. It will provide educators with a common language on which to base their program development and should permanently establish the school library resource center as an equal partner in the educational process. This work will be greatly facilitated by a collaborative partnership between classroom teachers and teacher-librarians.

Integration of Educational Technology

All levels of our school system have been greatly influenced by the growth of educational technologies. Computers are used for word processing, desktop publishing, information storage and retrieval, multimedia presentations, instructional presentations, the reinforcement of skills, motivation, and the promotion of literacy. As well, CD-ROM, the Internet, and the World Wide Web offer educators great opportunities to expand the educational experiences they provide students. Nowhere has the impact of educational technologies been felt more strongly than in the school library resource center.

Many teacher-librarians took the lead in using computers in an educational setting when they embraced computers as powerful management tools for the operation of online public access systems. These OPAC systems allow teacher-librarians to manage a school's resources more efficiently and accurately, as well as providing school library resource center users with freer and easier access to the collection. The result is that teacher-librarians in many schools have become very knowledgeable about automation of resource center collections and the use of computers for word processing and in the instructional setting. This expertise has added a leadership role to their responsibilities in the school because they find themselves assisting classroom teachers in becoming familiar with the many useful roles computers have to play in preparing students for an information age.

Although teacher-librarians have embraced the management role computers can play in operating a school library resource center program, they also realize that the use of information technologies is best developed within an overall plan for information literacy rather than in isolated computer programs that teach computer literacy as a separate set of skills. This gives the collaborative partnership between classroom teachers and teacher-librarians a new focus as they plan for the incorporating of information technologies into the development of information literacy. As resource-based units of study are planned, both partners will find many opportunities to use CD-ROM programs, electronic encyclopedias, and computer databases as sources of information for students. The information skills and strategies needed to physically and intellectually access information in traditional print formats transfer easily to the new electronic media, which also have the added advantage of being strong motivators for student involvement. As these educational technologies become more pervasive within our society, the demand will continue to grow for their integration into the daily instructional experience of all students. If classroom teachers and teacher-librarians work together, they can greatly facilitate the development of meaningful programs that use information technologies to their fullest potential.

Promotion of Literacy

Benefits also accrue when classroom teachers and teacher-librarians share the responsibility for promoting literacy within their school. Together they create a learning environment in which a love for reading flourishes and the value of writing is nurtured. Literacy development involves reading and listening to, writing and speaking about, "real" literature. Teacher-librarians have always found opportunities for literature-based instruction, and whole language has brought literature alive in the classroom.

Sharing literature and spreading its influence throughout all aspects of education has enabled classroom teachers and teacher-librarians to plan for literacy promotion and development in ways that excite students and motivate them to read for personal enjoyment and for their informational needs.

The Goal of Lifelong Learning

When individuals take responsibility for their own learning, they develop important attitudes and skills that enable them to learn independently throughout life. Educators more than any group realize how much we are constantly learning. We take new courses, develop new curriculum, implement new programs, learn new technological skills, and recognize that we never stop learning. Infusing students with this sense that learning never ends but continues throughout life must be the ultimate goal for all educators.

Processing information and reading and enjoying literature will ensure that we help produce "literate" individuals who are at ease with information in its various forms. In this so-called information age, it is becoming increasingly important for individuals to cope with the proliferation of information that surrounds and bombards them. Sorting through the quantity of information that is out there and critically choosing the relevant information needed to solve problems will require individuals who are rich in literate experiences as well as capable processors of information. The development of these literate individuals will be assured when teachers and teacher-librarians share this responsibility and carefully plan for the development of the skills and attitudes that are essential for independent, lifelong learning.

Summary

With the demands of the information age and the changes in teaching/learning theory and practice, a new role for the school library resource center has emerged. No longer used simply as a storehouse of materials, the school library resource center is a dynamic and well-stocked central resource, operating a program that is fully integrated into a school's curriculum and is based on greater cooperation between classroom teachers and teacher-librarians in the planning, development, implementation, and evaluation of resource-based units of study. The partnership is rooted in shared expertise in curriculum development, knowledge of students, and the effective use of resources plus a mutual commitment to the provision of a more meaningful and rich teaching/learning environment.

The benefits of this redefined relationship allow for more effective use of resources and instructional time, as well as the integration of educational technologies, the promotion of literacy, and the pervasive goal of lifelong learning.

CHAPTER TWO

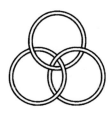

ACTIVATING THE PARTNERSHIP

With a rationale established and an overview of the role of the school library resource center in place, we look now at the major components of the program. First, a sound working model for learning is outlined in a discussion of resource-based learning. Then the collaborative planning, teaching, and evaluating process is described as the way the partners bring about a resource-based learning program. The information process provides a consistent framework within which classroom teachers and the teacher-librarian activate their partnership, develop independent learning skills, and promote lifelong learning.

If the partners in the learning process are to come together to bring about a richer environment for the development of information literacy, several major features must be in place to ensure that a good working model is achieved. First, a learning strategy must be in place that all the partners agree to and that will move the school's overall learning goals ahead. This learning strategy will be based on the school's philosophy and reflect current understandings of how learning takes place. It will be rich in good-quality resources and give the learner lots of opportunities for input into the learning. It will be a consistent strategy in which classroom teachers and teacher-librarians can use and combine their areas of expertise to give the learners a meaningful and enriched learning environment. It is resource-based learning that becomes that learning strategy. Second, a process must be established for implementing resource-based learning. This collaborative planning process facilitates the designing, developing, teaching, and evaluating of learning activities that allow students and teachers to meet their information literacy goals. Third, there must be an understanding of the information process so that a consistent plan for developing information skills and strategies can be designed.

 # RESOURCE-BASED LEARNING

What Is Resource-Based Learning?

Resource-based learning is an educational model that is the principal learning strategy applied by teacher-librarians whenever they want students to use resources to develop their information literacy. Classroom teachers use resource-based learning as one of a wide repertoire of teaching methodologies that they draw upon when planning a fully developed and balanced curriculum. Resource-based learning is defined as a "planned educational program that actively involves students in the effective use of a wide range of appropriate print, nonprint and human resources" (Ontario Ministry of Education, 1982). It allows educators to integrate resources into activities that develop the skills and strategies needed to use information effectively.

Several key points emerge out of this definition. First, resource-based learning is *planned*; classroom teachers and teacher-librarians meet and decide what students will learn, what resources they will use, and how they will use those resources to best meet the learning outcomes. Second, resource-based learning *actively engages students* in the learning process. Students are not passive receivers of information or of someone else's meaning; they actively interact with the information and develop their own understanding. Third, resource-based learning develops the skills that students need to be *effective users of information*. Students learn to be wise planners, to ask good questions, to locate the right resource for the task at hand, to access the information they need within the resource, and to critically evaluate that information. Finally, resource-based learning engages students in the use of *a wide range of resources*. Students and teachers do not rely solely on the course textbook or the assigned readings; they seek out and use resources that represent different opinions and experiences, that reflect various learning styles and abilities, and that extend classroom learning experiences.

Resource-Based Teaching or Resource-Based Learning?

Educators frequently confuse resource-based learning with resource-based teaching, which simply means a variety of resources are used to enhance instruction. Within the resource-based teaching concept, it is quite possible for students not to be actively involved in the learning process even though the teacher has made good use of print, nonprint, or human resources. Curriculum-related materials, such as trade books, videos, and computer software, as well as information gathered from guest speakers from the school or the community have become an important aspect of good teaching. Most teachers and teacher-librarians will agree that even though they employ these resources in their instruction, it is impossible to guarantee that every student interacts with the resources in a meaningful way. This is because the teacher, rather than the student, is at the center of the learning environment. The teacher decides what content and concepts are important, how they will be presented, and how students will learn them. If the teacher presents key content and concepts with the assistance of a video, filmstrip, or multimedia software, some students will be highly motivated to view and listen to the information, while others will be less interested and less receptive to the lesson.

Teachers may attempt to evaluate how well their students have learned by asking questions that require discussion or writing or some other appropriate response. When this evaluation reveals that objectives have not been successfully realized, educators look for alternative methods to reteach or remediate. All too often the student continues to remain passive and uninvolved in the learning process despite the teacher's efforts. Resource-based learning attempts to have students interact with resources that are chosen to meet their abilities and learning style.

There will always be a place for direct teaching that is enriched with the wise use of good resources. However, by placing students at the center of the learning environment and having them make greater decisions about their learning, a more meaningful involvement in the learning process is guaranteed. This implies more than simply putting resources and students together in the classroom or the library-resource center. That will only ensure physical access to resources, whereas resource-based learning demands that students have intellectual access to resources as well.

What Happens in Resource-Based Learning?

Intellectual as well as physical access to resources is essential for resource-based learning to occur (Haycock, 1991). This means that the resource must be appropriate for the student. If the reading level of a print resource, such as a book, magazine article, or study print, is beyond that of the student, interest and understanding will be hampered. Likewise, nonprint materials, such as videos or computer software, may contain information that is either too simple or too sophisticated for the student. A guest speaker may have an impressive body of knowledge but may not be able to convey it in a way that will be meaningful for the student.

Both teachers and students need to be actively involved in the selection of appropriate resources. The teacher and the teacher-librarian identify and examine the best available resources and together they decide how these resources will be used by their students. Do they provide the information students will need? Do they meet the ability needs of the students? Do they reflect a variety of learning styles? Individual students then choose the resources that they are able to understand and that appeal to their interests, needs, and learning styles. Learning becomes more personalized and relevant as students develop skills and strategies for extracting and processing information.

Careful planning ensures a variety of independent and collaborative activities. Groups or individual students may be engaged in resource-based learning activities in a variety of locations. However, the emphasis is always placed on the interaction that occurs between the student and the resource. This interaction may happen during an activity in which groups of students are examining artifacts in order to make observations that will be recorded on a chart. A student may be independently reading part of an encyclopedia article and writing point-form notes on a fact sheet or grid. Students may need to locate specific resources in the school library, or they may use a learning center filled with a variety of resources that is located in the classroom or the school library.

Learning stations are another option for structuring resource-based learning. Specific skills and resources are included within a series of structured activities. Attractive work areas are created to house the resources and establish a place for small groups to work. Students rotate through the learning stations processing the selected information by using appropriate information skills and strategies. This approach is particularly effective with older students.

How Do Teachers Facilitate Resource-Based Learning?

A shift in teaching style is necessary when resource-based learning occurs. Classroom teachers and teacher-librarians do less directing and more facilitating as they actually move from the center stage of the learning environment to a more supportive, guiding role. Direct instruction will be necessary at times, and the textbook may also be the most appropriate resource for a teaching or learning activity.

Resource-based learning is another form of the many prevalent teaching strategies common in cooperative learning, holistic learning, and other child-centered methodologies. Classroom teachers simply add resource-based learning to their repertoire of teaching strategies. Although resource-based learning is an alternative strategy for classroom teachers, it is the pervasive strategy

employed by teacher-librarians to bring students and resources together in meaningful ways.

Many of these facilitative teaching strategies are accused of being haphazard or even chaotic in their development of the learning environment. Resource-based learning is neither. Using resources that are physically as well as intellectually accessible requires a highly structured learning environment and even more planning. This planning and cooperation amongst the partners in the learning process become the critical factors for success. Since the partners plan and work together to facilitate learning by guiding and tracking students through key learning processes, greater attention is given to individual student needs. It is also possible to ensure that learning objectives are being met because a variety of assessment methods may be used, such as conferencing, checkpoints, learning logs, and observations. Greater accountability is also possible for students, who become more aware of their personal responses to the learning processes. Journals, learning logs, and other forms of self-evaluation are also useful in evaluating how well the learning objectives are being realized.

When teachers and teacher-librarians share responsibility and commitment for developing information literacy, they work collaboratively to plan for resource-based learning opportunities at all grade levels. Those opportunities that incorporate one or several subject or curriculum areas may evolve into a school-based plan, which will ensure that all students benefit.

 # OWLS: A Resource-Based Unit of Study

Introduction

In an effort to provide an example of what a resource-based unit "looks like," this brief description is given of one such unit completed by fourth-grade students.

Resource-based units of study may be shorter or longer than this particular one. They may include any subject area as a starting point but usually bring in many other curriculum areas. Units that receive this much planning are usually repeated each year, with adjustments for different students and new resources. Not all units are written up in this much detail, but a brief record of what went on in the unit is always important to keep for reuse and adaptation of the unit in the future. We are particularly concerned with listing the general concepts we want to develop, describing the specific objectives in the content area, and outlining the skills and strategies we want to teach. The activities tend to center on a major writing project or a multimedia presentation.

Checkpoints are built in along the way to provide students with feedback on their progress. These checkpoints are short conferences that allow us to help students with their individual difficulties, as well as identifying areas for mini-lessons that groups may need before proceeding any further. Evaluation focuses on the process first, so students

know that this process is ongoing, developmental, and an essential part of their literacy skills. The product is evaluated in terms of the specific goals set out for the students.

All teachers approach the process in different ways, with different goals in mind. The teacher-librarian tries to establish some consistency within and across grade levels in the areas of resource-based learning and the development of information skills. They keep abreast of the curriculum being used and constantly search for ways to link it with the school's information skills continuum. Teacher-librarians provide leadership in developing teachers' and students' understanding of the information process and how it develops, which really helps in the use of a consistent language across the school and in developing the school library program across the curriculum.

This brief outline of one resource-based unit of study is not the only way it can be done. Each school and each school library program will develop unique methods for activating the partnership between the classroom and the school library resource center. The authors collaborated with Grade 4 teachers at Glen Stewart School to develop this particular unit of study.

Unit Overview

As an extension of a novel study on *Owls in the Family* by Farley Mowat, a class of 28 fourth-grade students became involved in a collaboratively planned unit of study on owls. Students were very interested in owls, and the classroom teachers

recognized this as an opportunity to activate the information process. It was seen as an opportunity for a process-oriented approach in which students would complete a short research report. The study would also be extended with an art activity.

Unit Goals

The generalized topic of "owls" will be explored through activities that

1. develop an understanding of the information process and how it is activated when we need information;

2. emphasize methods for organizing information into paragraphs;

3. provide the opportunity for students to prepare a short report; and

4. develop visual literacy by having students create pictures that emulate the style of Tejima's illustrations in *Owl Lake*.

Information Skills

The following information skills and strategies within the information process and taken from the Prince Edward Island Department of Education's *Information Skills Continuum* (1989) will be taught:

1. Use a book's title page and verso to identify author, title, publisher, and copyright date.

2. Use a book's table of contents to locate information.

3. Develop techniques to organize information.

4. Develop techniques to record information.

5. Write a content-related report that includes a title page.

Curriculum Areas

Language arts, science, and art.

Students

This heterogeneous fourth-grade group of 28 students have had these previous experiences:

a) exposure to a variety of print and nonprint media;

b) an introduction to note taking in third grade;

c) introduction to the parts of a book and how they are used;

d) information-gathering activities related to a third-grade theme on "birds";

e) using the creative thinking process of brainstorming;

f) preparing short information reports on animals (third grade).

During the planning process that preceded this resource-based unit, the following list of responsibilities was divided between the classroom teacher and the teacher-librarian.

Classroom Teacher's Responsibilities

1. Outline for students the expectations for the unit of study.

2. Hold a conference with students at the checkpoints along the way.

3. Provide reinforcement on note-taking and information-organization skills.

4. Provide time for students to read materials available in the information station organized and located in the library.

5. Assist students as they collect and record information and then organize the information into categories.

6. Assist students as they complete an art activity.

Teacher-Librarian's Responsibilities

1. Collect resources and set up an information station on owls in the library.

2. Give students an overview of the steps in research.

3. Teach students how to use the fact sheet established as a data gathering device (see appendix B).

4. Teach students how to organize their facts into categories that then become their paragraphs.

5. Hold a conference with students at the checkpoints along the way.

5. Assist the classroom teacher in the editing and revising of the reports.

6. Prepare the materials and the art activity to be used with the book *Owl Lake*.

Schedule

All activities were completed using consecutive days of two six-day cycles.

1. Introductory lesson: One-hour class. The classroom teacher introduced the unit and what would be happening. Teacher-librarian gave an overview of the information process. Students created "thought" webs on owls to activate their prior knowledge and to stimulate their thinking of the sorts of questions they would answer in their investigation of owls.

2. Preliminary lessons: Three one-hour classes. The book *Owls* by Lynn Stone (1989) was used as the main source of information for students. Sections of the book were put on overhead sheets to teach students how a table of contents, a glossary, and an index work. Then students began collecting information on their fact sheets. Classroom teacher and teacher-librarian circulated amongst the students, assisting them as they read the information and decided what the important facts were that they should record. The emphasis was on processing the information and recording facts in point form.

3. Organizing the information: Two one-hour classes. Students took the facts they had collected and organized them into categories. Students read over their facts and put together facts that went together. The classroom teacher or the teacher-librarian met with students as they decided on their categories and justified what facts went into each categories. At this checkpoint students had to have the teacher or teacher-librarian sign their organizing sheet as a signal that they were ready to move on in the process.

4. The writing process: With their information organized, students began rough drafts of their reports. After two one-hour writing sessions most students began to revise and edit. The class was split in two, with classroom teacher and teacher-librarian each taking a group for editing and revising their reports. This marked a second checkpoint, where the teacher and teacher-librarian met with students on their rough draft and signed the rough draft when they were ready for their good copies.

5. Sharing the information: Students then prepared their good copies. Throughout the writing process, emphasis was on keeping the information organized into paragraphs. After they completed the good copy, the students had to submit all their rough work, including their "thought" webs, fact sheets, organizing sheets, rough drafts, and their good copy.

6. Art activity: After the reports were finished, students spent two 90-minute periods completing an art activity that arose

from the reading of *Owl Lake* by Tejima. Students enjoyed the reading aloud of this picture book, and the discussion that followed focused on how the illustrator created the sense of peering into the nocturnal life of the owl. Students went on to create their own picture using oil pastels covered with a thick wash of black tempera. During the next session, they used sharp tools to scratch out pictures of owls at night. This allowed the bright colors of the oil pastel to "shine through." The results were very effective and demonstrated to students how difficult it was for the artist to create his pictures.

Results

Students really enjoyed this unit of study—they have such a natural curiosity about owls. The classroom teacher and the teacher-librarian reported that students wrote better reports because they had their data well organized before they started writing. By letting them develop their own categories (instead of giving them the categories) for their information, they established more ownership over the writing process. Having two teachers working on the process was also noted as very valuable. At the end students wrote some of their thoughts on the project and the processes it had activated.

 # COLLABORATIVE PROGRAM PLANNING, TEACHING, AND EVALUATION

Introduction

If resource-based learning is what students, classroom teachers, and teacher-librarians "do," the next question is: How do they do it? A process must be in place that will ensure that the development of information literacy will not be sporadic, erratic, or inconsistent. All students have the right to these experiences, and classroom teachers and teacher-librarians have the responsibility to bring these experiences alive. Therefore it is necessary to put in place a planning process that will bring the partners in the learning process together around the school's goals and objectives for information literacy. This process is referred to here as collaborative planning, teaching, and evaluation.

What Is Collaborative Planning, Teaching, and Evaluation?

Simply stated, collaborative planning, teaching, and evaluation is the process that involves teachers and teacher-librarians as partners in the development of curriculum that integrates resources, information skills, and shared program objectives. The partners plan, teach, and evaluate together activities that meet the interests and needs of students within the stated learning goals of the school.

What Are the Characteristics of Collaborative Planning, Teaching, and Evaluation?

Several characteristics must be stated to fully understand how collaborative planning works.

1. First, collaborative planning and teaching is a *process*. This implies that there are several operations to be completed—operations that interact with each other. Although the

components of the process can be isolated from each other, they are part of an integrated and dynamic process involving an equal partnership between the classroom teacher and the teacher-librarian.

2. For teacher-librarians, collaborative planning and teaching is the *pervasive* teaching strategy that they apply to all of their instructional activities. For classroom teachers, collaborative planning and teaching is an alternative strategy in a long repertoire that they activate whenever they need to use resources to develop literary appreciation and information skills.

3. Each partner in the planning process has particular *areas of expertise* to bring to the planning session. The classroom teacher knows the students' needs and the classroom curriculum. The teacher-librarian brings an expertise in resources, curriculum development, and information skills. The student brings enthusiasm for active learning and a sense of responsibility for meeting outcome expectations.

4. This process is focused on developing *student-centered activities* that are facilitated, monitored, and evaluated by both the classroom teacher and the teacher-librarian. Students make choices, organize plans of action, and make informed decisions about their learning. They are also actively involved in assessing their own learning.

What Are the Factors for Successful Implementation of Collaborative Planning, Teaching, and Evaluation?

In schools where collaborative planning, teaching, and evaluation are not prevalent, there are several factors that will ensure that the process develops easily. No one of these factors will singularly guarantee success, but together they represent the sort of conditions that exist in schools where cooperative planning, teaching, and evaluation is working well.

Flexible Timetable

In many school libraries, a rigid timetable is still in place in which the teacher-librarian spends the whole day slotted into a cycle of classes that provide a time for book exchange and likely a second period for teaching library skills. This type of schedule restricts the purposeful teaching of information skills and limits the access classroom teachers have to the school library and the teacher-librarian when they are working on class projects. A flexible timetable is essential if the teacher-librarian and the classroom teacher are going to be able to plan a series of library times to bring resource-based learning to their students. For example, the time needed may be one-hour periods each day for a week. The teacher-librarian can book this time for that teacher and his or her students. This ensures consistent application of students' time to the available resources,

motivates them to complete the work quickly, provides a concentrated effort to really teach the information skills well, and keeps everyone from getting bored or bogged down with the project. The teacher-librarian and the classroom teacher will be able to teach the information skills (including the traditional "library skills") during this block of time, and more importantly the skills will be taught and practiced within a strong context and an immediate purpose. The teacher-librarian manages the timetable so that each class receives a balance of the available time for their resource-based units of study.

Book exchanges can be handled in a variety of ways. Some school libraries have technical support staff to circulate books to students. Automated school libraries make it easier to control signing books in and out. Students can sign their own materials in and out with ease when there is a barcode system in place. Student monitors and parent volunteers can also help run a circulation system that frees the teacher-librarian to teach. Some school library resource centers have "open" book exchange times that could start before the first bell in the morning or afternoon or at designated blocks of time throughout the day.

Adequate Staffing

It may seem obvious to state that no school library resource center program will operate within the framework of collaborative planning, teaching, and evaluation without the services of adequate staff in the library, but it is amazing how many school libraries try to operate with a bare minimum of staffing. The school library resource center will only be a room full of books without a well-trained teacher-librarian.

Some standards and guidelines suggest that for every 350 students there should be at least one full-time teacher-librarian. This standard leaves many school libraries woefully understaffed. A full complement of support staff, including library technicians and clerks, will also ensure that the teacher-librarians will be able to be teachers and not be forced to spend all of their time in the management of the facility. It is important to note that clerks and technicians should only be employed to assist, not to replace the professional teacher-librarian.

Many school libraries are limited to part-time teacher-librarians, many of whom are itinerant and must service two, three, and even more school libraries. Although it is true that some teacher-librarian time is better than none, increasing staff for the school library must be a major priority for all educators if we are to prepare students for their rightful place in our information society.

In some cases, the automating of the school library facility is seen as a way of replacing or limiting the professional position of a teacher-librarian with less expensive technicians. This thinking as well needs careful reconsideration. Although technology is viewed as an important asset and in reality an essential part of the school library resource center program, it must be remembered that access to information needs a human interface. Students and classroom teachers need more than terminals, clerks, and masses of data; they require instruction and leadership in developing the skills and strategies needed not only to access information but to use it in intellectually critical and effective ways. Technicians and computers can ensure physical access to resources, but only a teacher-librarian can teach and ensure that intellectual access will be achieved.

Administrative Support

Teacher-librarians who operate highly successful school library programs constantly attribute a large part of that success to the strong support given to the school library by their administrators. These administrators recognize the vital role school libraries play in today's education, and they go out of their way to provide adequate staffing, adequate budget, and a shared vision for the school library. The first partnership that the teacher-librarian needs to foster is the one with the school's administrators. When this partnership is centered on a shared vision for information literacy and the goal of lifelong learning then the school library program seems to take off. Together the teacher-librarian and the school administrator articulate the vision to the staff, and they develop a plan of action that will see the principles of resource-based learning, collaborative planning, teaching, and evaluation, and the integration of the information process develop over the course of several years. Staff recognize that this vision has administrative support and that it has been incorporated into the overall plan for learning for their school.

Planning Time

To develop the process of collaborative planning, teaching, and evaluation, teacher-librarians and classroom teachers need adequate planning time, both during the school day and after school. This time allows the partners to decide on the goals and objectives for the resource-based unit of study, to identify the information skills they wish to teach, to design the activities their students will do, and to build in evaluation tools. Planning time is necessary for any job to be done well, and teaching is no different.

A Plan for Information Skills Development

Each school library needs to develop its own plan for information skills development that meets the stated learning goals of the school. This plan develops when a school's staff members decide what information skills they feel are appropriate for each grade level. They decide when to introduce a skill and lay out a series of developmental steps to achieve mastery of the skill. Many school districts and provincial departments of education have skills continuums that schools use as a guide as they are developing their own school-based plan. Developing such a plan ensures that classroom teachers and teacher-librarians feel a sense of ownership for the teaching of these vital information skills.

What Are the Components of the Collaborative Planning, Teaching, and Evaluating Process?

Any process can be broken down into a series of steps or procedures that guide the process and ensure that nothing is left out. The planning process outlined here is very similar to traditional models of lesson planning familiar to most teachers. Schools usually develop their own planning guides, which help keep a record of the planning session but more importantly act as a focus for the planning process, making sure all points are covered and that the most efficient use is made of valuable planning time.

The *identification of goals* and objectives is a basic starting point. Some teachers prefer to brainstorm on the general topic and then begin to narrow it down to specifics, whereas others are very comfortable going straight to the identification of goals and objectives. These goals must be stated in terms of general and specific learning outcomes and often begin with the phrase "Students will." The goals combine the learning objectives of the classroom teacher's program and the information goals found in the school's information skills continuum. Expectations for students' demonstration of learning should also be clearly stated.

Many try to *identify the resources* that will be needed or will best suit the learning objectives. Attention must be paid to providing a variety of resources to accommodate different learning styles and ability levels. The discussion around resources often leads to suggested learning activities that would use the resources effectively. In some cases, the discussion begins with ideas on the type of activities the partners would like to engage the students in, and then teachers search for resources that will help them set up these learning activities. In either case, the discussions centering on resources to be used will be lively and lengthy.

Preparing the learning activities will take up a large part of the planning process, involving both teachers equally. One might prepare a learning station to be located in the library resource center, while the other prepares one to be used by students in their classroom. Someone will prepare booklets for the students while the other sets up an information station to house all the learning resources needed for the unit. The variety is endless and will require several meetings by the partners to go over how the preparation of materials is developing. Built into all learning activities are lots of opportunities for open-ended activities, choices for students, and informed decision making about how they will complete the activity—these are not to be fill-in-the-blank types of sheet work!

Planning for who will teach what, how the timetable will be organized, how the students will be organized for the activities, and *how the unit will be managed* usually happens while the learning activities are being developed. Each partner shares the teaching, and students are organized either into small groups for instruction, kept together as a whole class, or asked to work individually to complete their work. Sometimes one half of the class will be with one teacher for instruction, while the other teacher takes the other half for a second activity. Then the groups switch. Sometimes both teachers are working with the whole class at the same time, or one person keeps the whole class while the other meets with individuals for a conference or a mini-lesson. This partnering of the classroom teacher and the teacher-librarian is often given as one of the strong points of this whole process because it allows for an adjustment of the student/teacher ratio and it encourages alternate teaching strategies.

Once the management aspects are finalized, decisions have to be made as to the *assessment procedures* for the unit. Some system has to be developed for tracking student progress through the learning activities. Evaluation is not left totally to the end but is an ongoing part that is built into the whole learning experience. Both the classroom teacher and the teacher-librarian are active in the evaluation process, either with each one monitoring progress in particular aspects or by each tracking the same components and then comparing notes afterwards. Students are kept well informed of how they will be evaluated and are given clear messages about what is expected of them. Checklists, mini-conferences, checkpoints, learning logs, response journals, journals, and mini-tests are only some of the evaluation techniques used by classroom teachers and teacher-librarians during resource-based units.

It is also important to plan for the sharing or *celebration of the learning* that has taken place. These activities are exciting culmination events that include the students, their teachers, and the parents in meaningful opportunities to learn from each other and share what has been happening. These events could be part of the final evaluation but are usually meant as positive ways of reinforcing the love of learning.

At the end, the classroom teacher, the teacher-librarian, and the students should sit down and evaluate how well the learning developed and list the strengths and weaknesses of the learning activities, as well as all suggestions of ways to improve the unit. These sharing times are also vital in setting the next set of learning goals and planning future resource-based units.

What Tools Are Available for Tracking the Collaborative Planning Process?

The following collaborative planning guides (figures 2.1, 2.2, and 2.3) provide a visual outline for the partners to follow as they prepare resource-based units. There are many formats that could be followed, and the ones here can be adapted by individuals to meet their own instructional styles and planning needs.

(Text continues on page 35.)

PLANNING GUIDE #1

Theme or Topic

_____

Time Line

_____

_____

Learning Objectives

_____

_____

_____

_____

_____

_____

Learning Resources

_____

_____

_____

_____

_____

_____

_____

Learning Activities

_____

_____

_____

_____

_____

Evaluating the Learning

_____

_____

_____

Fig. 2.1. Planning Guide 1.

PLANNING GUIDE #2

Title of Theme or Unit of Study _____

Grade Level _____   **Number of Students** _____

Titleframe _____

Brainstorming on the Topic:

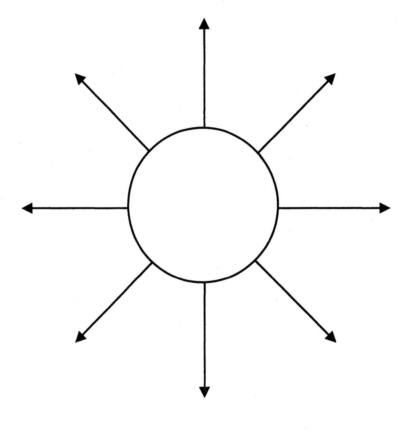

Fig. 2.2. Planning Guide 2.

(Fig. 2.2. continues)

LEARNING OBJECTIVES

Students Will...

_____
_____
_____
_____
_____
_____
_____
_____
_____
_____
_____
_____
_____

LEARNING RESOURCES

_____
_____
_____
_____
_____
_____
_____
_____
_____
_____
_____
_____
_____
_____
_____
_____
_____

Fig. 2.2. (continued)

(Fig. 2.2. continues)

LEARNING ACTIVITIES

_____
_____
_____
_____
_____
_____
_____
_____
_____
_____
_____
_____
_____
_____
_____
_____
_____
_____
_____
_____
_____

EVALUATING THE LEARNER

_____
_____
_____
_____
_____
_____
_____
_____
_____
_____
_____
_____
_____
_____
_____
_____

Fig. 2.2. (continued)

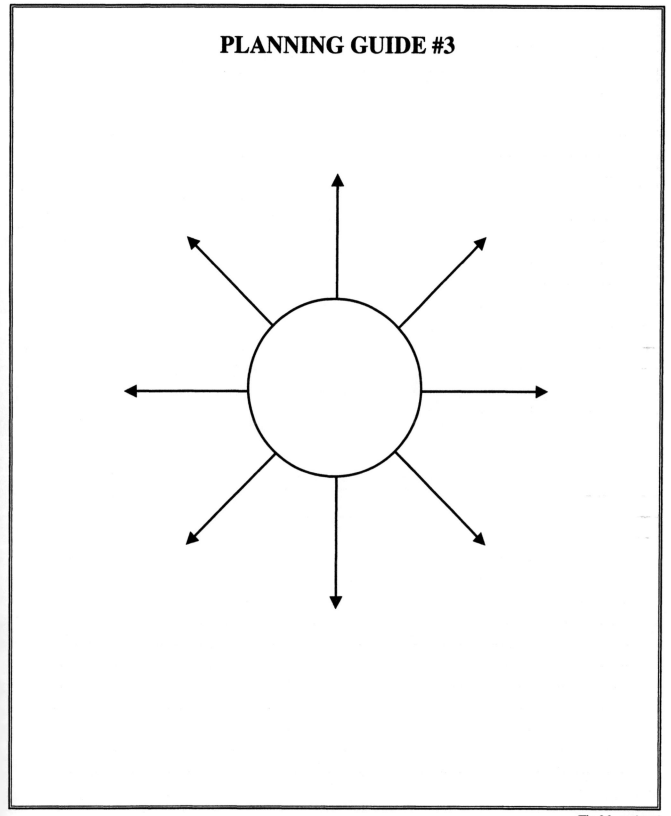

PLANNING GUIDE #3

Fig. 2.3. Planning Guide 3.

(Fig. 2.3. continues)

Topic (theme, unit) _____ Grade Level _____

Date _____ Teachers _____

Goals: (Why are we doing this?) _____

_____

_____

Learning Objectives: (What specifically do we want students to learn? Content/Concepts)

_____

_____

_____

_____

_____

_____

_____

_____

_____

_____

_____

_____

_____

Information Skills: (from the school or district continuum)

_____

_____

_____

_____

_____

_____

_____

_____

_____

_____

_____

_____

_____

Fig. 2.3. (continued)

(Fig. 2.3. continues)

Resources: (print, non-print, human)

_____

_____

_____

_____

_____

_____

_____

_____

_____

_____

Activities: (grouping, locations, responsibilities of each teacher, time...)

_____

_____

_____

_____

_____

_____

_____

_____

_____

_____

_____

_____

_____

_____

_____

_____

_____

_____

_____

_____

_____

Fig. 2.3. (continued)   (Fig. 2.3. continues)

Evaluation: (How will the learning be tracked? Who will do the evaluating?)

_____
_____
_____
_____
_____
_____
_____
_____
_____
_____

Notes for Future Reference: (How could this project be improved? Are there better resources to teach the skills? What is the feedback from students?)

_____
_____
_____
_____
_____
_____
_____
_____
_____
_____
_____
_____
_____
_____
_____
_____
_____
_____
_____
_____

Fig. 2.3. (continued)

THE INFORMATION PROCESS

Introduction

Educators have believed for a long time that students need to do research as part of their educational experience. Traditionally this research has been generated by the teacher's desire to have students do a "project" on a certain topic related to their larger overall curriculum plan. These projects tended to be annual events within their program and always followed a similar pattern to the way the activity was done the year before.

This conception of research is flawed in several ways. First of all, students have little input into the timing of the activity, the content of the subject matter, the purpose of the project, and what the final product will be like. Usually, these research projects are conducted outside the context of the classroom when students are assigned research projects to be completed on their own and passed in within two or three weeks. As well, teachers provide little guidance through the process and students choose to regurgitate facts that are often copied verbatim from encyclopedias. All of these factors combine to make the research project a dreaded event in the life of many students.

Throughout the 1980s, educators have recognized the need to focus more attention on the processes involved in learning and to balance the place of the final product within the context of the entire learning process. This realization has had dramatic effects on the way we teach the language arts. We treat reading and writing as interconnected components of an interactive process and have developed many teaching strategies that focus on literacy processes. We challenge students to develop a set of skills and strategies that work for them. We emphasize meaning and purpose, avoiding the traditional teaching of skills in isolation far removed from their "real-life" applications.

However, for many educators, the research project continues to remain an isolated event that may appear integrated because it is focused on a particular theme but still has as its primary goal the production of a written report. We need to reevaluate how we engage students in research so that we focus more on the process-oriented approach, which makes the product a natural result of the whole process.

What Is the Information Process?

The information process is defined as a problem-solving process involving decision making as well as critical and creative thinking. Learners are active and in control of the learning while engaged in developing a set of skills and strategies for planning, gathering, interacting with, organizing, creating, sharing, and evaluating information. The partners collaborate to provide opportunities and support for resource-based learning, which includes the development and practice of appropriate information skills and strategies.

What About "Research"?

The word *research* is defined by Webster's as "a careful, systematic, patient study and investigation in some field of knowledge, undertaken to discover or establish facts or principles." This definition implies that a plan is needed to carry out such an investigation; the plan involves some systematic procedure in order to be successful; it is a search for information and for understanding; it implies a discovery will take place, an uncovering of some new "meaning."

This description is far from the way research projects are conducted in most classrooms. In many cases, students are expected to conduct research on familiar subjects like "animals," which is one many of them already know a lot about. What new knowledge is discovered? What new understandings are acquired? What new information is gathered? For the most part, students are asked to fill in an outline, often provided by the teacher. They are asked to find information on an animal's appearance, its habitat, its reproduction (usually called Babies or Young), its food, its enemies, and its defenses. Children have no thinking to do, no plan to make; they simply fill in the blanks and then write it up. It's no wonder their written reports all sound the same, are full of short choppy statements, draw no conclusions, and are often copied word for word from a book or printed from a computer screen. It is obvious we are missing the point if we continue to have students work in such meaningless ways. Is there not a process involved that we need to facilitate and guide students to acquire? Is this sort of "research" so ingrained in our thinking that it is impossible to think of it in any other way?

It seems clear that we have to focus students on the process that is involved and develop teaching strategies that will foster the growth of students' ability to develop a hypothesis, investigate a topic, and present their results in a meaningful way. We need to broaden our frame of reference to recognize that this process is primarily about information, all of the ways we use information, and the critical thinking skills necessary to process that information effectively.

Any text we use to engage students at school, whether it be in the language arts, mathematics, social studies, science, or art, involves an interaction with information. In reading, writing, listening, speaking, viewing, and presenting, processing information is the major learning activity, in which the learner creates "meaning" out of their interaction with the text. If we define "research" as part of this holistic process, we will integrate the information-seeking process into the entire context of our curriculum and not leave it as an isolated event that happens once or twice a year.

When we combine the reading/writing process with critical thinking strategies, what emerges is a new concept, *the information process*, which engages students in a meaningful interaction with information to achieve the goals of acquiring new knowledge, of thinking critically and creatively about that information, and of constructing a deeper understanding of important concepts. This information process is the framework for developing students' information literacy.

What Are the Characteristics of the Information Process?

The information process can be described in terms of several characteristics that are similar to other learning processes and are important to help us clarify our understanding of how this process works.

1. First of all it is a *process*. This implies that it involves a particular method of doing something with several operations interacting at the same time. One part of the process builds on a previous part and lays the groundwork for the next.

2. This process is *developmental*. It cannot be mastered through one teaching activity or one project. Students develop their understanding of the operations involved in the process, practice the specific skills needed to ensure growth, and develop strategies that they can apply when they meet similar situations in the future. Each grade level in school builds on the previous one, with everyone cognizant of the holistic picture involved.

3. It is *pervasive*. Information touches all aspects of the teaching/learning environment, and the development of skills and strategies to process information efficiently and effectively are developed across the curriculum. The information could be about an author, a particular genre, a content area subject, the rules of phonics, spelling, prewriting, or any other learning activity. Working with that information to make meaning and then sharing that information happens in all aspects of the curriculum.

4. The process is *dynamic*. This process is not static or lifeless; there is an action involved. Students are actively engaged in the learning; they are not passive observers. It is vigorous, with an energy of its own that moves the activity from point to point.

5. It has a *metacognitive component*. Students need to be consciously aware of what they are doing and where they are going next. We need to talk to them about the components of the process and what they mean. The more students can tell what they are doing and how they are doing it, the better able we are to tell that they really internalized the learning.

6. It is *inclusive of other learning processes*. No learning process operates in isolation from others. The information process includes the processes of reading, writing, and creating. At any one time, a student will be reading a text, observing a phenomenon, creating new information, recording notes, writing or sharing information. All of the learning processes are brought together within this one process.

What Is the Reading/Writing Connection?

Throughout a vigorous debate over the past twenty years, educators have discussed what reading is and how best to develop it with students. The role of phonics, concepts like emerging literacy, whole language, cooperative learning, shared reading, and invented spelling have all emerged out of this debate. If a definition of reading is possible, it would probably be defined as a "meaning-making" process involving the interaction of phonemic, syntactic, schematic, and semantic structures. The focus is on the processes that lead the reader to understanding the printed message and not on the reading of words isolated from the context in which they get their meaning. Learners are active and in control of the learning situation. It is their job to develop a set of skills and strategies that enables them to read for enjoyment and to read for information. The teacher facilitates this process by providing a rich literate environment full of meaningful, purposeful opportunities for learners to interact with text.

Our recent recognition of writing as a process that develops over time and in partnership with the reading process has had more impact on the teaching/learning environment than any other single educational development. Educators no longer wait for reading to reach a certain developmental point before introducing students to writing. The two processes develop simultaneously and in partnership, with a consistent focus on process, not just product, and with an overall emphasis on meaning. Writing can be defined as a "meaning-giving" process involving the interaction of phonemic, syntactic, schematic, and semantic structures. Again the learner is active and in control of the learning. The learner develops skills and strategies in prewriting, drafting, revising, editing, and publishing. The teacher acts as a facilitator and guide, building a rich, literate environment in which students feel comfortable and willing to take risks.

The information process embraces both the reading and the writing processes and focuses on answering questions. Critical and creative thinking skills are nurtured here with a major emphasis on problem solving. Questions like: How do animals adapt to their environment? Why do people build homes? What are ecosystems? and Where in the world would you find deserts? are the launching points for investigation and study. Students make decisions about where they will find the answers to their questions, how best to record their answers, and how to share with others the information they found. Although it is impossible to isolate the processes from each other, there are certain points in the information process when reading, viewing, and observing are the major activities, and then later writing, creating, and presenting take over.

What Are the Components of the Information Process?

Just as it is possible to outline the writing process into the major components of prewriting, drafting, revising, editing, and publishing, so too can the information process be broken down into major parts that fit together to form a framework for processing information. Teachers help students learn what this framework is and encourage them to develop a set of skills and strategies that will enable them to activate this framework whenever they work with information. The following is a list of the major components of the information process:

1. planning and initiating the process;

2. gathering the information;

3. interacting with the information;

4. organizing the information;

5. creating new information;

6. sharing the information;

7. evaluating the process.

Each component can be examined individually to analyze what role it plays in the overall process. Each is important and cannot be eliminated. While planning to activate this process with students, teachers may want to emphasize certain areas, but at the same time no aspect will be left out. Although the components are outlined in a linear format here,

it is important to note that the process is really circular, beginning with the planning but coming full circle to evaluating the process, which leads the students to new questions they wish to answer, and so the process starts again. Figure 2.4 represents how we can envision the process.

Implied in this model is an understanding that students may go back and forth from one component to another. For example, after gathering some information students will interact with it and then decide they need to go back and gather more information. Similarly, while creating information, students may find they are missing some information and have to go back to interacting with information to fill in the details. In addition, evaluation is ongoing and not left entirely until the end of the whole process. The following chart (fig. 2.5) gives an overview of the components of the information process and some of the key skills and strategies covered in each phase.

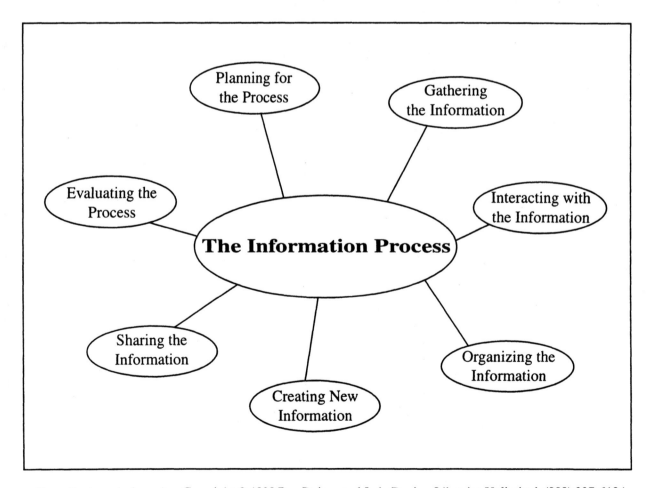

OVERVIEW OF THE INFORMATION PROCESS

STAGES   **PROCESSING STRATEGIES**

Planning for the Process   Establish topic
                                    Identify audience and presentation format
                                    Establish evaluation criteria
                                    Review the whole information process

Gathering Information   Identify information sources
                                    Locate resources
                                    Collect resources

Interacting with the Information   Read, view, observe, etc., the information
                                    Choose the relevant information
                                    Evaluate information
                                    Record sources of information

Organizing the Information   Organize information into catagories
                                    Collect more information to fill in gaps
                                    Organize catagories into outlines

Creating New Information   Writing process and/or
                                    Making process and/or
                                    Photographic process and/or
                                    Artistic process and/or
                                    Speaking process and/or
                                    Dramatic process

Sharing the Information   Review procedures for presentation
                                    Prepare a product for presentation
                                    Apply language conventions
                                    Reinforce audience etiquette

Evaluating the Process   On-going component
                                    Review component
                                    Self-evaluation
                                    Review/reflect on the information process

Fig. 2.5. Overview of the Information Process.

What Do Students Do Within Each Phase?

A closer examination of each of the major components is needed to clarify what students are doing within each phase. Each phase can be broken down into several operations that are the primary focus at the time. Drawing students attention to what these operations are will help them see a process unfolding—a process that will guide them on their search for information.

Planning for the Process

A major part of students' problems occur because they are not aware of the planning they need to do to ensure success with the information process. They often realize they need to choose a topic or try to define their question, but they leave out other parts and run for a book without thinking about the whole process.

In the planning component, *deciding on a topic* is the first objective. This can be chosen by the student or assigned by the teacher, but it needs to arise from some purposeful activity that students have been involved with in class. Most often classrooms are organized around some theme or general topic that is providing the major focus for the learning that is happening at the time.

For example, several classes of sixth-grade students were working on a pioneer theme, and after a great deal of reading and writing activities students were asked to choose a topic of interest that they were to pursue in more detail. Several major subject areas were identified, and students held a class discussion on the subjects. Afterwards they came up to large sheets and wrote their name under the topic that was the most interesting to them. The diagram in figure 2.6 shows how they looked.

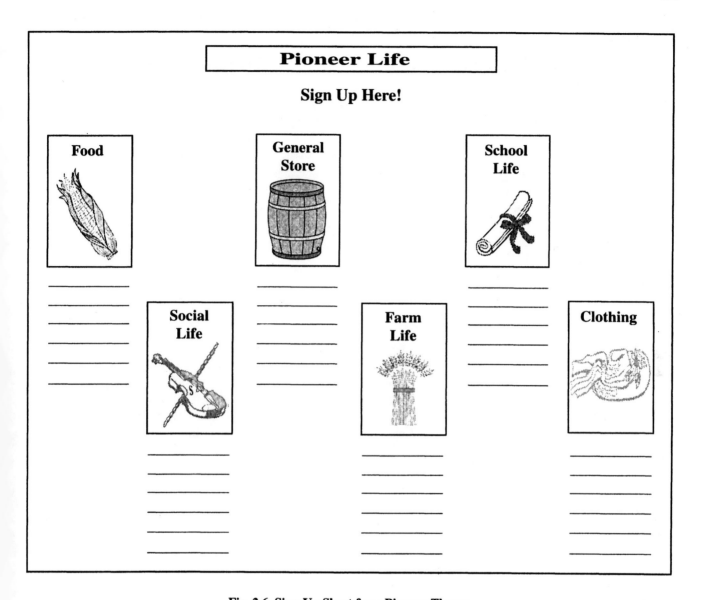

Fig. 2.6. Sign-Up Sheet for a Pioneer Theme.

Once the general topic is decided, it is critical to spend some time clarifying the topic or research question. Students often wind up searching for information on too general a topic without really narrowing their question down to a manageable size. What is it exactly that you want to know?

Continuing the example from above, students who signed up for each general subject area had a group discussion and brainstormed to list all the possible topics related to that subject. Figure 2.7 shows some they included.

Students were then able to choose a more specific topic, such as "preserving food in pioneer times." This format allows for a lot of group discussion, which is important for facilitating students thinking about their subject. It also provides plenty of choices for the students while helping the teacher maintain some control over the topic area. This format is not the only one available, but it works well in large classes that are evolving into more student-centered environments.

Fig. 2.7. Subtopics Developed in a Group Discussion.

Having chosen a topic, students then spend some time brainstorming on their specific topic to *determine their prior knowledge* on this topic. They should complete this on their own and then share it with someone who could help spark other ideas. Students need to decide what they already know about this topic. Then they are better able to decide what they need to find out. Too often, they are spending time looking for information they already know when they should be looking for new information or at least looking to verify what they already know. Time spent in this section is always time well-spent.

A simple thought web like the one pictured in figure 2.8 is a basic strategy that can quickly become part of any student's repertoire of thinking strategies. Students are often amazed at how much they know already. It also is valuable to point out ideas they have that may need to be verified, because we all have so many misconceptions about so many areas.

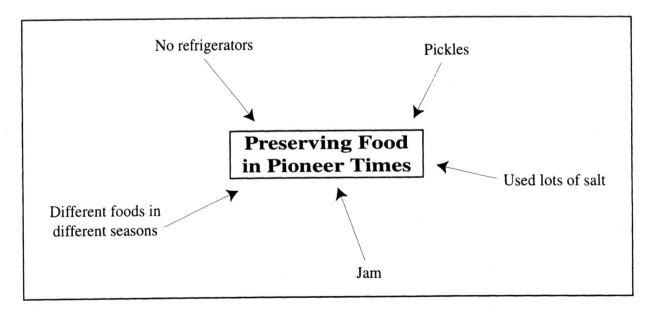

Fig. 2.8. Thought-Web for Pioneer Food Topic.

TOPIC: Preserving Food in Pioneer Times

1) How did they preserve their food?

2) What foods did they preserve?

3) What did they use to preserve food?

4) Do we use any of the same methods today?

5) How long could they save food?

6) Where did they save food?

Fig. 2.9. Student-Generated Questions on Pioneer Topic.

With their web completed, students may *develop a list of questions* on their topic. This list should include lots of who, what, where, when, why, and how questions based on the thought web and their earlier discussions on the general topic. Sometimes it is necessary to *organize the questions* into categories or key words that will help later with the information search, but this is determined by the complexity of the topic and the maturity of the students. Figure 2.9 shows the questions one student developed for the "preserving food" topic.

Students now know their topic well and are prepared with a list of specific questions that will direct their information search. However, the process is not so rigid that these questions won't change. Certainly they will and often do. But students learn that as they get into the information search, the information they are finding may lead them in a different direction. They may want to come back to this step in the process and rethink their topic in light of the information they are able to find.

With their list of questions in place, some *decision on the end product* may be valuable here, not to predetermine what everyone must do but to give some perspective on how much time will be spent, who the audience is, the teacher's expectations, and the products students may be keen to produce. The actual information that students find often will determine how it can best be shared, and any final decisions on the end product may have to be made later.

As a final part of this "Planning for the Process" component of the information process, it is critical to *review the other phases in the process*. Students should review the gathering, interacting, organizing, creating, sharing, and evaluation steps that they will go through for the rest of the process. It gives them an overview of the whole process so they will recognize where they are in the process and where they are going.

Gathering the Information

At this point, students are ready to start their search for a variety of information sources that will help them answer their questions. In order to efficiently and effectively access information sources, they apply a variety of skills and strategies that help them find information and then to access the information within the resource. It is helpful if they make a plan for information gathering, which would involve activating the traditional location and retrieval skills usually associated with a library. They would then activate their plan by applying the skills associated with using indices, tables of content, fact files, and other book parts useful to access the information.

The Information Gathering Plan

With the list of questions in place, students can develop a list of possible subtopic headings, keywords, or categories and then a list of the possible sources of information that they could try. Some of the more common sources include:

- Card catalog or OPAC
- Specialized reference materials
- Personal journals and letters
- Encyclopedias (print or electronic)
- Audio-visual materials
- Dictionaries
- Computer software
- Personal interview
- Pamphlets, brochures
- Atlas, maps

Activating the Information-Gathering Plan

The plan provides direction for the most likely sources of information, but to use the plan students need skill in finding the information within the sources. This is a two-fold process in which they first locate the resource and then find the information inside the resource. For example, using the Online Public Access Catalog to locate nonfiction books involves certain skills; finding that book on the shelf requires other skills; and once the book is located, other skills in evaluating or assessing the resource and in using the parts of a book are necessary to access the information. There are several organizational tools within a resource that help us find the information we want. Some of these tools include:

- Index
- Fact files
- Outlines
- Table of contents
- Chapter summaries
- Guide words
- Bibliographies
- Cover
- Glossary
- Book jacket

Subject headings and key-word lists are all helpful in accessing the information in any resource. With a plan for gathering information, students don't waste time thumbing through a resource hoping the information will jump out at them. They can use the plan and gain access to the resource with more purpose.

Interacting with the Information

Now that they have some information sources in front of them, students are ready to find the information they want. All of their reading skills will be needed here. They have basically three operations to complete: (1) interact with the resource; (2) record any relevant information they may find; and (3) record the sources of information they have used.

Interact with the Resource

Students are now at a critical point in the process. If they have not been given some understanding of the process, they are very likely at this point to start copying text from the resource they have just located. They need to understand that interacting with the resources requires that they read, listen, view, touch, observe, interview, and so on, at a level of understanding sufficient to identify relevant information from the resource. It is critical to be sure students cannot only physically access the resources that are provided, but that they can also intellectually access the resource. If they cannot comprehend the text, the habit of copying will surely be reinforced.

There are two major operations at this point: choosing relevant information and evaluating the information found. The following are appropriate strategies for choosing relevant information:

- skimming
- scanning
- following headings and subheadings
- reading charts and diagrams
- interpreting maps, graphs, and pictures
- QSR (Question, Skim, Read)
- SQ3R (Survey, Question, Read, Recite, Review)

While evaluating the information, the following skills or strategies are appropriate:

- distinguishing between fact and fiction
- distinguishing between fact and opinion
- determining accuracy
- checking currency
- identifying author's point of view
- determining any bias

Recording Relevant Information

While students are interacting with the information, they need a system for recording the important facts they will need later. This note taking has traditionally been modeled by teachers as the point form, but students need to be encouraged to develop their own system for taking notes. Different research questions demand different forms; different skill levels of students will also determine what format will work the best. Figures 2.10, 2.11, and 2.12 present several formats students find helpful.

Fact Sheet
Subject: PIONEER FOOD

- meat came from hunting	
- preserved food in salt	
- made their own flour	
- baked their own bread	

Fig. 2.10. Fact Sheet.

A Data-Gathering Chart

	Homes	Food	Travel	Beliefs	Family	Others
Micmac						
Huron						
Iroquis						

Fig. 2.11. A Data-Gathering Chart.

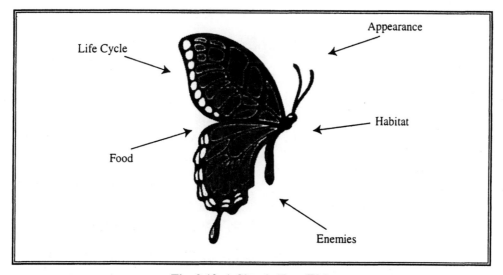

Fig. 2.12. A Simple Fact Web.

Record the Sources of Information

Students need to learn at a very early age that it is important to give credit where credit is due when it comes to sources of information. Even in the early primary grades, students can record the basic information on a book—author, title, publisher, and year of publication. Emphasis should be on the principle and concept of recording sources of information rather than strict adherence to a particular bibliographic format.

Organizing the Information

With their data-gathering device full of information taken from a variety of resources, students need to spend time organizing the facts so that they can be used effectively in the creating and sharing parts of the process. This phase encompasses strategies required to categorize and structure the data gathered while interacting with the resources. They are basically assembling the data into new patterns.

This categorization will allow students to identify any missing facts they may have to go back and find before moving on. The categories also become the guide for making an outline, writing a rough copy, making a display, or whatever they decide to do during the creating and sharing processes.

This process involves having the students read over their facts and find two that "go together" for some reason. Once they can link two facts, they look for a third or fourth fact, tell what is common about them, and call them a category. Often these categories are similar to the questions or keywords from the planning stage. Then they search for other facts that may go into that category. This process of finding related facts and grouping them goes on until all the facts are used. Most often there are some left that don't fit in any category. Some children call these "Other Interesting Facts" or exclude them. Figure 2.13 shows one outline that students could use to organize their facts into categories. Once a diagram like this has been completed, students can easily identify any gaps in information and then can go back and find more information to complete all categories.

Gathering Food	Festival Foods
Hunting for Food	Preserving Food

Fig. 2.13. Data-Gathering Chart with Categories of Information.

Creating Information

This phase involves taking the raw data collected and giving it life. No longer limited to the traditional report writing, students readily accept the challenge to create all sorts of stimulating and exciting methods of sharing information.

Any combination of these processes will be used at this phase:

- the writing process
- the speaking process
- the making process
- the photographic process
- the artistic process
- the dramatization process

This combination of creative processes makes for some very exciting activity for students. It allows them to decide what is the best way to share the information they found. It may need to be presented in a very visual and powerful way or in a more subdued, academic format. Choice is important; student input is critical; and a focus on the creative process involved will lead to more positive results. Appendix C provides a partial list of some alternatives to the traditional research report that students could use to share their information.

Sharing the Information

Information sharing is concerned with the development of effective presentational techniques. Students need support to practice their sharing skills so that information will be shared in the most interesting and informative way. The major skills and strategies associated with this phase include

- the language conventions associated with preparing a product for presentation
- the techniques of sharing information effectively
- the etiquette of being a good audience

Students respond very positively to presentation techniques that have a high visual impact. Written reports need to be integrated into larger presentations that include drama, art, and displays, and oral reports are never boring, repetitive readings of the same report from everyone. Practicing their presentation should be encouraged, and modeling of what makes a good presentation is very important.

Being a good audience is a skill we rarely focus on in school, yet we demand it from our students. So many of us have "laid down the law" just before a visitor to the class or a guest speaker arrives. More time to practice being an audience will greatly improve attention skills. So too will teaching the proper behavior for an audience. Preparing presentations with the audience clearly in mind will likely have the greatest impact.

Evaluating the Process

Evaluation plays a pivotal role in the information process. Although it is listed last in the cycle, it is not left until the end. Evaluation happens throughout the process as well as at the end. There are two major components:

Ongoing Component: While the activity is happening, students and teachers evaluate the process and the product.

Review Component: After the work is complete, teachers and students identify strengths and areas where improvement is needed.

A variety of strategies well known to most educators can be employed. Teachers recognize the need to focus their evaluation on the process and to look at product within the context of the whole information process. Students are encouraged to evaluate their own development of the skills and strategies necessary to be efficient processors of information. The following is a short list of some evaluation techniques that meet this criteria:

Observation: Teachers observe students' comments, questions, group interaction, discussions, use of time and materials, etc.

Journal/Daily Log: Students record activities they are working on, list questions they may have, evaluate their own progress, express opinions, etc.

Collecting Materials: Students collect samples of their work to provide a profile of growth and development.

Checklists: Teachers and students use checklists to monitor progress; to serve as a record of skills and strategies introduced, developed, and maintained; to provide checkpoints along the way; etc.

Student Self-Evaluation: With practice students can use simple formats to evaluate their own performance of various components of the information process.

Peer Evaluation
Conferences or Interviews with Student: Same as with the reading/writing process.
Questionnaires and Inventories
Tests and Quizzes

THE INFORMATION PROCESS IN ACTION

Author Study Guide

One of the most common literature projects that students pursue at both the primary and intermediate grade levels is the author study. Within literature-based programs a great deal of emphasis is placed on developing a sense of what authors do and how they do it. Teachers and students often seek biographical information on the author of a book they may be using for a whole class novel study, a literature circle, a text set study, or an individual reading. This provides an opportunity to apply the information process in a structured and formal way. It allows the teacher to teach how the information process works while taking everyone through an author study. It provides the perfect chance for the teacher-librarian and the classroom teacher to activate their partnership around a resource-based unit of study.

The "Student's Guide to Completing an Author Study" (figure 2.14) was developed over several years of trial and error with students and teachers. It works much like an advanced organizer that guides students through a fairly structured experience with the information process. It includes the major components of the process and has three checkpoints built into it where students meet with teachers. Students have found the checkpoints very helpful since they prevent them from getting too far behind or from getting lost along the way and then having to backtrack. Teachers like the way it keeps them focused on the process. Classroom teachers just starting to develop a partnership with the teacher-librarian find this guide provides a focal point for their work together. It outlines the skills and strategies they are trying to develop and encourages the partnership of classroom teacher and teacher-librarian in the planning, teaching, and evaluating of resource-based units of study.

After such a formal "instructional" application of the information process, students are better prepared to activate the process on their own. They can see each phase outlined in a simple way and how it can be applied to any subject area. Our work with this outline has shown that it is helpful as a direct teaching tool, and we find students are transferring the learning they have done through the author study to other investigations or studies they have completed. Readers are encouraged to adapt this guide to their own situations.

(Text continues on page 58.)

Student's Guide to Completing an Author Study

Student's Name_____   Grade _____

Teacher's Name _____   Date _____

The Information Process

STEP 1	Planning for the Process	• Stating your purpose, naming your subject, listing questions...
STEP 2	Gathering Information	• Locating sources of information
STEP 3	Interacting with the Information	• Reading, viewing, and recording the information (making notes...)
STEP 4	Organizing the Information	• Catagorizing your notes, making an outline
STEP 5	Creating New Information	• Writing a biography, illustrating
STEP 6	Sharing the Information	• Reports, displays
STEP 7	Evaluating the Process	• Student's evaluation, teacher's evaluation

Fig. 2.14. Student's Guide to Completing an Author Study.

(Fig. 2.14. continues)

STEP 1 • PLANNING FOR THE PROCESS
—Stating your purpose, naming your subject, questions

1. Why are you doing this? _____
    _____
    _____

2. Who is the subject of your author study? _____

3. Use this space to create a "web" about your author.

```
  ┌──────────┐        ┌──────────┐        ┌──────────┐
  │          │        │          │        │          │
  │          │        │          │        │          │
  └──────────┘        └────┬─────┘        └──────────┘
         ⇘                 ⇓                 ⇙
              ┌─────────────────────┐
              │    Author's Name    │
              └─────────────────────┘
         ⇗                 ⇑                 ⇖
  ┌──────────┐        ┌──────────┐        ┌──────────┐
  │          │        │          │        │          │
  │          │        │          │        │          │
  └──────────┘        └──────────┘        └──────────┘
```

4. What are the major categories for your questions about this author?

    _____   _____   _____

    _____   _____   _____

    _____   _____   _____

    _____   _____   _____

(Fig. 2.14. continues)

Fig. 2.14. (continued)

STEP 2 • GATHERING INFORMATION
—Finding sources of information

1. What sources of information will you use?

   Meet the author AV kit   Blurbs on the author's books

   Special books on the author   Pamphlet or brochure

   Encyclopedia

   Other sources _____

2. My Plan for Gathering Information

   _____

   _____

   _____

   _____

   _____

****

STEP 3 • INTERACTING WITH THE INFORMATION
—Reading, viewing, recording your information (making notes)

1. How will you record your information?

   _____

   _____

   _____

   _____

   _____

   _____

(Fig. 2.14. conti

Fig. 2.14. (continued)

FACT SHEET

(lined blank form)

Fig. 2.14. (continued)

(Fig. 2.14. continues)

ORGANIZING YOUR NOTES

_____   _____
_____   _____
_____   _____
_____   _____
_____   _____
_____   _____
_____   _____
_____   _____
_____   _____

_____   _____
_____   _____
_____   _____
_____   _____
_____   _____
_____   _____
_____   _____
_____   _____

_____   _____
_____   _____
_____   _____
_____   _____
_____   _____
_____   _____
_____   _____

**CHECKPOINT #1 After you have organized your notes,
have a teacher sign here.** _____

(Fig. 2.14. continues)

Fig. 2.14. (continued)

STEP 4 • ORGANIZING THE INFORMATION
—Catagorizing your notes, making an outline

1. Read over your notes carefully.

2. Write your notes again and put them into catagories. For example, put all the notes about "early life" into one group. Use the blank organizing sheet to help you organize your notes.

3. Use the catagories to help you make an outline.
   MY OUTLINE FOR _____

1. Major Heading _____
   _____
   _____

2. Major Heading _____
   _____
   _____

3. Major Heading _____
   _____
   _____

4. Major Heading _____
   _____
   _____

5. Major Heading _____
   _____
   _____

6. Major Heading _____
   _____
   _____

**CHECKPOINT #2 Meet with your teacher after
              your outline is done.** _____

(Fig. 2.14. continues)

Fig. 2.14. (continued)

STEP 5 • CREATING NEW INFORMATION
—Writing a biography, illustrating

1. Use your outline to write your *first draft*.
    Remember Try to write a good opening sentence.
    Each new heading from the outline means a new paragraph.

2. Read your first draft. Make any revisions you can.

**CHECKPOINT #3 Meeting with a teacher about your
    rough draft.** _____

3. Write the *second draft*. Make the changes you were shown from the first draft.

4. Read your second draft and make any improvements you need. Someone else may give you a suggestion as well.

5. You should be ready for the *final draft*.
    Remember This should be your very best work. Be Neat!!!

6. Write your sources of information on a separate sheet.

****

STEP 6 • SHARING THE INFORMATION
—Reports, displays

1. How will you share the information? _____

    _____

    _____

2. Use the list as a guide to getting ready to share.

    - Read over your final copy.
    - Check for your name.
    - Did you include sources of information?
    - Could you answer questions about this author?

    - Color your illustration.
    - Do a nice cover.
    - Is this your best work?

(Fig. 2.14. continues

Fig. 2.14. (continued)

STEP 7 • EVALUATING THE PROCESS
—Student's evaluation, teacher's evaluation

Student Evaluation:

Use this space to reflect on the information process you have just completed. Use the
space provided to write your feelings about how well you did with this activity.
These questions may help you:

> What did you learn about the information process?
> What did this author study teach you about your own writing?
> What things did you do really well?
> With what things do you feel you need help?

_____
_____
_____
_____
_____
_____
_____
_____
_____
_____
_____
_____

PROJECT CHECKLIST

Here is a list of all the things you are expected to have completed for this author study.
They are meant to be a guide for you to be sure that you get everything done.

Please pass in:
    This author study booklet
    All rough drafts
    Your final report

You need teacher signatures for:
CHECKPOINT #1 _____
CHECKPOINT #2 _____
CHECKPOINT #3 _____

Fig. 2.14. (continued)

Summary

The information process as outlined in this part of chapter 2 provides all educators with a framework in which to ensure that learners develop effective and efficient skills and strategies necessary for the completion of an information search. It provides a common language for teachers and students to use when dealing with information, and it allows students flexibility in developing their own set of skills and strategies that meet their interests and abilities and suit their learning styles.

We have attempted to establish a rationale based on the realization that looking for information is a process, a process that incorporates reading and writing and the basic creative and critical thinking strategies that form the foundations of education.

The components of the information process were outlined to clarify what happens when we engage in any information processing. A specific example related to the traditional author study was also provided.

We are in an information age. As educators we have recognized information literacy as a basic component of the teaching/learning environments we establish for our students. To ensure that students develop strong information literacy skills we need to build on the framework for the information process given here so that we will be able to provide our students with rich information-based experiences that will help them develop the skills and strategies they will need to function as literate adults.

Having outlined the goals of information literacy within the context of resource-based learning and having shown how to achieve those goals through the process of collaborative planning, teaching, and evaluation, we turn our attention now to providing the partners in this process with examples of this dynamic partnership in action.

CHAPTER THREE

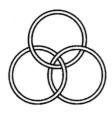

THE PARTNERSHIP AT WORK

In this chapter, examples will be given that demonstrate how the partnership among teachers, students, and the school library can result in dynamic and innovative learning experiences. The activities and projects described here have been used with elementary students from L.M. Montgomery School and Glen Stewart Elementary School on Prince Edward Island. They resulted from collaborative planning sessions with our staffs and provide a sampling of our students' daily experiences within their school library resource center program.

In the daily operation of the school library resource center, students and teachers have many incidental opportunities to visit it for their individual purposes. Students or teachers may need to look a word up in a dictionary, find information in an electronic encyclopedia, get a picture from the picture/pamphlet (vertical) file, return materials, check out materials, pick up a piece of AV hardware, or meet someone. There are dozens of reasons to go to the school library resource center, but if the most effective use of the school library is to be made, then planned learning experiences like the ones outlined here are essential.

As classroom teachers and teacher-librarians develop their understanding of resource-based learning and begin the collaborative planning process, it is helpful to "see" examples of how other sets of partners have developed these principles. This chapter describes what this partnership looks like when it has been activated and provides several examples that readers may wish to adapt for their own teaching/learning situations.

Activating the Partnership

Whenever students need learning resources for pleasurable reading or for information, opportunities exist to activate the partnership between the classroom and the school library resource center. Classroom teachers may initiate the partnership as they begin the planning process for a new theme or unit of study. The teacher-librarian may seek the partnership in anticipation of special upcoming events or curriculum topics. In most cases, a school-based plan for resource-based learning and information-skills instruction will develop in direct response to the teaching styles of the staff, the administrative support for the program, the leadership provided by the teacher-librarian, the outside influences of district policies, and the demands of the community. It should not be left to happenstance or informal and isolated instances; rather it needs to be incorporated into the overall school-based plan for instruction.

In smaller schools, planning time for the teacher-librarian and classroom teachers of a particular grade level can be programmed directly into the timetable so that the partners come together regularly to plan for the next resource-based unit or theme. Other schools may find it difficult to arrange a timetable that will allow all the classroom teachers at a particular grade level to plan during the school day. After-school time will be needed, as well as planning sessions throughout the school day when part of a grade level may be free for follow-up or more specific planning. The old adage "where there's a will, there's a way" holds true for most situations and reflects the attitude that in most cases if planning is considered important, time can be found for it.

Opportunities to Partner

Most examples of classroom teachers and teacher-librarians working together with students fall into one of the following categories:

1. meeting the demand for resources;

2. advocating and developing literacy;

3. activating the information process.

It is also likely that these activities will not be developed in isolation but will involve an integration of two or more under a theme or unit of study.

For example, if a theme is being developed on the environment, many resources will be needed, students will work on certain information skills, and many poems and stories related to the theme will be shared. The teacher-librarian and the classroom teacher can plan and teach several lessons that will develop skills and strategies in one, or all, of these areas. Other themes may center on encouraging students to read a particular genre or on promoting poetry and may involve only one or two shared lessons for the partners. Whatever the focus, the opportunities for the partners to come together are endless.

This chapter includes several examples within each category of projects completed by students. These examples reflect what happened when classroom teachers and their teacher-librarian came together to meet the demand for resources, to promote literacy, and to collaboratively plan, teach, and evaluate resource-based units of study. These examples worked for the students for which they were planned and within the context of the school library resource center program that exists in our two schools. They are not prescriptions to be followed rigidly, but rather they act as models for others to adapt. They are described here with the hope that they may help other educators as they develop their own integrated school library program based on the principles of information-skills development, collaborative planning and teaching, and resource-based learning.

 # MEETING THE DEMAND FOR RESOURCES

In most educational programs today, some resources are provided with the program and others must be supplied by teachers, both to supplement and to fully realize the intended learning outcomes of the stated curriculum. This implies that just as planning for teaching of skills and strategies must be ongoing and built in to the curriculum process, so too must there be planning for the provisioning of resources. Acquiring resources and making them accessible to teachers and students must be part of the overall plan and must be integrated into the development of the school curriculum. Two general categories of resource provisioning are discussed here: resources for independent use and resources for instructional purposes.

Materials for Independent Use

A large part of the role of the school library is to provide students and teachers with a wide variety of materials easily accessible to them and that will meet their needs for reading for pleasure and reading for information. Students find these materials on the shelves in the school library or by visiting displays of materials set up by the school library. Choosing books and signing them out are basic activities for all students.

Book Exchanges

Book exchanges operate in all school libraries, but no two schools handle them exactly alike. Traditionally these times were managed solely by the teacher-librarian and usually in isolation from the literacy program in the classroom. Now, teacher-librarians are placing more emphasis on the teaching component of their role and have developed many alternate strategies to handle the management of book exchanges for students.

Classroom teachers as well have reexamined their roles in promoting and encouraging reading with their students. More and more they recognize their role in helping students select reading materials. They realize the importance of choice reading, and they know students need many more reading materials than the traditional once-a-week book exchange allowed. Classroom teachers want their students to have greater accessibility to the school library collection, and they recognize the significant role they play in the development of positive attitudes among students towards the school library.

The whole language philosophy has as a basic tenet the need for a wide range of good quality resources to build a literacy program that will nurture literacy acquisition in a natural and risk-free environment. This too encourages the school library resource center to be more responsive to the immediate needs of whole language classrooms by offering flexible, open book exchanges that allow students to come individually, in small groups, or with their teacher and the whole class to choose books. They come when there is a real need for materials, not just because it is their turn in the timetable to visit the school library.

Along with these differences in the roles of classroom teachers and teacher-librarians have evolved a variety of strategies that allow the school library to open up the schedule for the choosing and exchanging of materials throughout the school day. With **open book exchanges**, students may come for materials at any time of the day. Classroom teachers design a plan to manage their students' use of library time. Some may allow students to go at any time, whereas others choose the first and last part of the day as more suitable. Some teachers make daily visits with their classes, some alternate days for half the class, and some let students choose a large number of books and keep them in the classroom for a few days.

The use of a **library pass** system has also been successful in monitoring individual and small-group access to the library. Each class may have several passes that are taken by the student or students when they visit the library. They are placed in a small card pocket in the library while the students are there and then returned with them to the classroom. It is a quick way of checking who is in the library while providing the classroom teacher with some control over who is in and out of the room. These passes also encourage student independence and promote accountability.

The biggest difference in moving to an open book exchange format is in the attitude of students towards choosing books. Those who are avid readers are thrilled to have more accessibility to the collection. Many students with reading difficulties start to make daily visits and sit and read or take a book home. The school library becomes a more relaxed and social place where students share books they have just read, talk about ones they didn't like, or "compete" to get their hands on the latest editions of popular favorites. Students and teachers both notice that more books are taken out of the library and that more books are being read.

Managing open book exchanges is not as difficult as it seems at first. The use of student monitors to handle the exchanging of materials works very well. Early in September students are trained in the circulating procedures, and then they are assigned a time in the library schedule that suits their overall timetable. In a very few weeks, these students are able to handle most situations, which leaves the teacher-librarian free for planning with teachers, teaching students, or helping them select materials.

Parent volunteers are also a valuable asset in the management of book exchanges. They are especially helpful during peak times like early morning and late afternoon, which are favorite times with students. Parent volunteers can often handle many other tasks related to circulating materials as well, such as pulling materials on specific topics, identifying items for repair, or adding new titles to the collection.

Open book exchanges also provide alternatives for school libraries that only have the services of a part-time teacher-librarian. Instead of using their limited time solely for book exchanges, part-time teacher-librarians can focus on the teaching component of their role while remaining assured that book exchanges will be well managed through the support of student monitors, parent volunteers, and a more integrated and effective involvement of the classroom teacher.

Computerized management systems also have a tremendous effect on streamlining the circulation procedures in the school library. The tedious job of keeping track of hundreds of book cards is eliminated; students only need a library card for signing out materials; better records of who has what book are kept; materials are signed in and out more quickly; students can find the books they want more easily. In many cases students are able to sign out their own materials and check them back into the library. The automated school library is much better able to handle open book exchanging, and it actually encourages students to sign out more materials.

Displays

The school library resource center has always been a place where students can see materials displayed in interesting ways. These displays are now playing an even bigger role in our programs because they can highlight parts of the collection, focus attention on a particular issue or topic, and encourage students to borrow more materials.

Students are very used to visiting displays in museums, theme parks, playlands, and even their local shopping malls. These displays are visually interesting, promote ideas, teach new concepts, and are designed to motivate interest on the part of the visitor. School libraries need to adopt some of these principles into the types of displays that are set up in the school library. They can be interactive, thought provoking, attractive, student centered, and full of interesting and exciting materials for students to view and borrow for their own reading pleasure. They may even be located in other parts of the school.

School library displays are usually set up to promote or celebrate a special event or to highlight materials on a theme that is being developed in certain classes. Usually materials in the display are on a reserved list and can be kept by borrowers only for a short time. This allows the material to circulate among a large group of borrowers. Some of the items in the display may not even be allowed to be removed because they are valuable or easily damaged.

Designing and creating displays can also be used as a teaching strategy by giving students the responsibility for setting up displays. They can find materials in the library on a topic, design the display around the space provided for them, and then work collaboratively to actually make the signs, arrange the items, and complete their display. Students respond positively to the challenge of making a display, and it's easy to elicit quality work because they know the display will be viewed by the whole school. The principles of good design and of making a visual presentation can be accented at this time. Classroom teachers often like to include creating a display as part of the final evaluation of an integrated theme because it encourages students to synthesize what they learned and then present to others what they know about their topic.

Materials for Instructional Purposes

In addition to providing materials for students' independent reading, the school library resource center is the central storing facility for many different types of materials used for instructional purposes by classroom teachers. In the past, this purpose was often the only link between the classroom and the school library, but now the partners recognize the need to find many more materials than before and to plan for the coordinated use of these materials. Although the teacher-librarian is the expert on what materials are available and how to best use them, the selection of appropriate resources is shared by both partners and forms a major part of the planning process. Teacher-librarians have developed many strategies to keep materials organized, accessible, and in good condition, and they search out better and better resources to meet the ever-increasing demands from teachers and students for the necessary support materials for learning.

Theme Materials

As classroom teachers and the teacher-librarian are planning, the topic of resources quickly develops as one critical to the success of the intended project. Teacher-librarians share and suggest materials appropriate to the topic, and together they choose ones that will meet the required need. These materials may be loaded onto a **book truck** and used in the classroom, reserved for the use of the students, or set up into an **information station** in the school library where students may come and get them as needed. Information stations act as displays for other students not directly involved in a theme and as a place to attractively house materials needed by students working on a particular topic. A **learning center** may also be built for a resource-based activity where students come to work independently with the selected resources on activities designed by the classroom teacher and the teacher-librarian. A **multimedia station** could also be established with a theme-related computer presentation available for student use.

The planning process also encourages setting up **theme boxes**, as explained earlier, as well as the keeping of a list of resources used for a particular theme. In this way, others may use the same list for their planning and items may be added to the list or deleted as new materials become available or old ones are weeded out.

Text Sets

With the growth of literature-based programs, many planning sessions focus on the provision of sets of novels that small groups of students need for a literature study. These **text sets** are usually stored in the school library and managed by the teacher-librarian, which helps to keep the resource in good condition and readily accessible for teachers when they need it.

"Text set" refers to two or more texts that are related in some way and used by the readers to share thoughts and feelings, to extend comprehension, and to search for reading and writing connections as they compare and contrast the related texts. Text sets are always arranged around a theme, topic, genre, or author. Whole class, small group, or individual titles are chosen to teach certain concepts and to develop particular skills and strategies.

To develop students' appreciation for literature and to provide them with a focus for using the text set, classroom teachers and the teacher-librarian include activities that nurture the reading/writing response. The response journal is popular, as is the response log, diary, or theme organizer. Students meet in small groups to talk about their feelings, reactions, and thoughts on what they have read. Many times they share their written responses or create new poems and stories to share. Text sets are an effective way to organize literary experiences and to provide independent, student-centered learning activities.

Nonprint Materials

Providing materials for instructional purposes is certainly not limited to books. There are many nonprint resources available to teach specific concepts that are stimulating and exciting for teachers and students to use. **Audio-visual software** that includes the traditional filmstrip, 16mm films, slides, and study prints has expanded to include many innovative **educational technologies**, such as CD-ROM, interactive databases, electronic encyclopedias, and multimedia presentations. These are the tools that students today demand to meet their information needs.

The school library is in the forefront of these technologies and is seen as the logical place for these materials to be housed and used. Teacher-librarians have quickly developed their expertise in this area because they were the first to realize the tremendous impact they can have on student learning. Students respond positively to most educational technologies and bring an open mind and natural curiosity to any activity centered on technology.

A consistent problem in the area of nonprint materials has been in the establishment of organizational procedures that allow for consistent and easy access to these materials. Most school libraries cannot afford the most expensive cabinets and shelving to do a proper job of housing this material. Strategies like theme boxes, subject portfolios, AV kits, etc., are examples of more informal methods of organizing nonprint materials and keeping them integrated into the common subject areas demanded by teachers. With the materials organized according to the theme they are normally used with, classroom teachers have greater access to all the related nonprint resources. Information on these materials can be stored in the library computer and their circulation handled through the normal procedures associated with books.

As themes are being developed, the teacher librarian may create an **information station**, which houses all resources on a certain subject, including print and nonprint. These stations are attractive and informative on their own and act as a focal point for the students and teachers needing these materials for some planned activity. The information station can be housed in the library, the classroom, or some other location in the school.

Human and Community Resources

Although print and nonprint resources continue to act as the main sources of information for students, teachers have always given firsthand experiences through the provision of a wide variety of human and community resources. Schools often design curriculum based on the valuable resources available locally. A nearby stream, a local factory, small and large museums, farms, businesses, and an infinite list of other wonderful resources should be included in any plan for resource-based learning. It is often the teacher-librarian who acts as the link between the school and the community, providing lists of people who are willing to come to the school and act as a resource person or who will provide demonstrations in school or on site. Community people also contact the school library directly, willing to provide information services for students and teachers.

In some areas, groups of community service agencies have banded together to publish lists of resource people and local sites that welcome school visits. They have even published binders containing a detailed listing of services they offer the community. With an increasing number of these community services available, it is critical to show students that such services are out there for them and that skills and strategies are needed to access them effectively.

Whenever planning for a resource-based unit of study, classroom teachers and the teacher-librarian need to include the use of these primary sources of information. Activities that have students contact these people and set up interviews, presentations, or field trips will help students develop strong communication skills as well as provide experiences tapping into community services. Students should act as the hosts when guest speakers are involved and thank them at the end.

Planning for a guest speaker or a field trip is also something in which students should have direct involvement. Many guest speakers know what it is like to speak to a poorly prepared group of student who were not given any prior knowledge or prepa ration for the whole event.

ADVOCATING AND DEVELOPING LITERACY

Sharing the Story

Teacher-librarians have always been concerned with literacy. Classroom teachers, students, and parents have consistently looked to the teacher-librarian for reading suggestions, and school libraries have been regarded as "reading centers." Our understanding of the role of the teacher-librarian is changing along with our understanding of literacy. Educational technology and immediate access to vast amounts of information are a wonderful reality for our students, and it has become important for teacher-librarians to promote both reading and technology. Definitions of literacy now automatically include "information literacy" along with the more traditional concept of reading. Educators agree that reading is not diminished in this information age; it has become more important than ever as students use such skills as skimming and scanning to choose appropriate information for their own needs. Critical thinking skills are also important as students learn how to evaluate and use the information they access. Teacher-librarians and classroom teachers have a shared responsibility for the development and promotion of literacy, which is an important and dynamic part of the school library resource center program.

There will always be a place for stories in the new "information center," although the methods for finding and sharing the story may change. When the educational partners work collaboratively, they are able to offer the best possible opportunities for literacy development.

Reading Aloud

The joy of story sharing is evident wherever people meet to talk about or listen to literature. Both classroom teachers and teacher-librarians enjoy reading books or selections aloud to their students. When an enthusiastic and sensitive approach is employed, students will eagerly participate. Much

has been written about the "how-to's" for success ful story reading (Barton and Booth, 1990), an many teachers and teacher-librarians have thei own secret formulas for reading with expression o creating suspense. However, less has been sai about the importance of finding the "right" story t read aloud. With a literature-based approach t teaching language arts, there is more emphasis o supporting the school curriculum with story read ing, rather than holding "story times" as isolate school library activities. When a class is workin; on a theme, the teacher-librarian and the classroon teacher will work together to choose literature tha reflects that theme. A particular literature genre o books by an author may be highlighted, and a stor reading activity may be planned cooperatively. Thi approach is quite different from the more traditiona one, in which the literature to be read aloud i chosen randomly or solely on the basis of th teacher-librarian's or students' preferences.

When story reading is planned to meet th shared objectives of the classroom teacher and th teacher-librarian, the possibilities for follow-up ar limitless. Although enjoyment is still the majo factor, reading aloud is clearly more than entertain ment and students learn far more than simple "bool knowledge." They become familiar with such term as author, title, illustrator, and characters, but mor importantly, they develop real appreciation for lit erature as an important part of life. Students becom discriminating listeners and readers as they are ex posed to a wide range of literature, and they becom increasingly independent as they are encouraged t read their own literature selections.

Many educators use technology to extend th read-aloud experience. The audio or videotape story may be used as a comparison or for addin; another dimension to literature sharing. Frequentl; the read-aloud activity is used to launch a theme o to provide the students with additional samples of the type of literature being studied by the class. When these activities occur in the school library resource center, students are reminded that the facility, the program, and the teacher-librarian are truly a part of their classroom curriculum.

Story Telling

Many classrooms and school library resource centers have special areas for story sharing. The "author chair" provides a focal point for reading aloud or storytelling. Teachers, teacher-librarians, and students read literature selections or their own writing or tell stories as others practice the skill of being good audience participants.

Although storytelling is often regarded as an art, anyone who can remember a story can also tell it. Visual aids, such as puppets, flannel boards, and overhead projectors, may be used, but these are not essential to bring stories alive for listeners. A desire to involve the audience and to add drama to the telling is all that is required to create a memorable sharing time. Many teachers and teacher-librarians invite guests to share their stories with their students. Volunteers, such as parents and celebrities from the community and, of course, other students, will welcome these opportunities to read or tell stories to students within the context of a classroom theme, a topical unit, or a special school activity. A good example of this type of activity is the local firefighter as storyteller who recounts a heroic rescue during a primary classroom's community theme. Senior citizens also have special stories rooted in their own memories, and this type of sharing experience can be rewarding and significant for everyone. When guest storytelling is planned to occur in the school library resource center, literacy development is shared with the community and the school's "information center" is viewed as a vital connection in its promotion.

Teacher-librarians and public librarians, who are familiar with vast numbers of children's books, often rely on their experience and memory to tell stories from those books. This method is particularly effective when picture book illustrations are used and the storyteller is able to retain eye contact with the eager audience. This type of storytelling is particularly appealing for children who have reading difficulty. They will gain the confidence they need to share their stories with others as the skill of retelling is modeled and the book's illustrations are shared and enjoyed.

Booktalks

Classroom teachers and teacher-librarians may involve their students in the promotion of reading through **booktalks**. Although the read-aloud activity is an excellent method for launching and supporting the literature-based theme or a unit of study, booktalking is equally effective and student participation is guaranteed. A booktalk is a presentation about a book, an author, or a group of books that someone is trying to convince someone else to read. Booktalks are usually short, highly entertaining, and interesting for the listeners—so much so, that they will want to read the books immediately.

Once the teacher-librarian models the booktalk, students will respond not only with great interest but also with a willingness to share their own reading through booktalks. Everyone enjoys hearing an introduction to a new book, with just enough information to inform listeners about the author and other titles by that author or within the same genre or topic. The plot summary sparks curiosity and interest, and the reading aloud of a selected passage will allow the audience to hear the author's voice.

Several books may be included in one session, and teacher-librarians often use this approach prior to an author's visit, as well as a thematic introduction. Students are then better prepared to make their own reading choices, and they also anticipate giving their own booktalks based on their reading. As they express their opinions about the books they are sharing, critical thinking is involved. When students answer others' questions about the book's readability or appropriateness as a thematic or genre choice, they will need to base their opinions on examples from the text and reflections on the author's style and purpose. The door will be opened for lively discussion; the enthusiasm generated by student booktalking is infectious. Classroom teachers and teacher-librarians have greater success in meeting their objectives for developing literacy when their students are provided with this type of framework for group discussion. As educators and students gain confidence and skill in booktalking, this activity may become very popular activity with everyone involved.

The "Guide for Booktalks" in figure 3.1 acts as a simple format for the classroom teacher or teacher-librarian who wants to give a talk on a particular book, genre, or collected works of an author. It has been written with the student in mind and has been used to guide them as they prepare to share books with their peers.

GUIDE FOR BOOKTALKS

The following is a multipurpose general guide to giving booktalks. Booktalks are an exciting way to involve the students in literature. Teachers and teacher-librarians may model this activity when they introduce a new theme, genre, or author. It is also a good way to provide students with information about available titles or text sets for independent reading or literature circles.

This method is easily adapted for students to present their own booktalks. It allows them to practice oral reading and speaking skills and to share their opinions and make recommendations. Teachers should use them as a way to evaluate students' understanding of genre and themes and to encourage literature discussion in the classroom and the school library.

Booktalks:

1) **Information About the Book:**
   Title:
   Author:
   Other titles in the series:
   Genre:

2) **Plot Summary:**
   Briefly describe the action in the story. Tell about the main characters and the setting as well. Don't reveal story endings!

3) **Read-Aloud Passages:**
   Select one or two passages to share. They should be about half a page in length. Choose descriptive and exciting segments.

4) **Related Titles:**
   What other books are good examples of this genre or theme? Is this book like any other you have read? Is it like any other that this author has written?

5) **Your Opinion of This Title, or This Genre, etc.:**
   Would you recommend this book to others? Why or why not? Is it a good example of this genre?

Fig. 3.1. Guide for Booktalks.

Book Buddies

Many elementary schools provide opportunities for older and younger students to share stories. The **Book Buddy** program is one approach that is easily initiated and maintained. Sometimes older students find books to share with younger readers and vice versa. They support each other in the reading experience and develop a strong friendship around books over the course of the school year. It is usual for two classroom teachers to combine their students by pairing the older students with younger book buddies. The teacher-librarian may contribute to the success of the book buddy program in several ways.

To facilitate the start of such a project, older students may visit the library resource center at the beginning when the class or small groups of students will have opportunities to prepare themselves to be good "buddies." Through role playing and discussion, the teacher-librarian encourages the students to think about ways in which they will become better acquainted with their younger partners. As they learn more about their interests and reading preferences and current classroom themes, they will soon be able to make good shared reading choices

for scheduled book buddy times. Sometimes classroom teachers prefer to have their first few book buddy sessions in the library resource center, where the teacher-librarian may also observe and assist the students with selection and sharing.

The charts in figure 3.2 and figure 3.3 offer tips for students who act as book buddies and who want help deciding on ways to make the experience positive.

The teacher-librarian's involvement with book buddies may extend beyond assistance with initiating the program and supporting students with the selection and sharing of stories. Classroom teachers are usually eager to strengthen the bonding that occurs between classes that have been paired as book buddies. The sharing naturally extends beyond the books that are read and enjoyed during the planned sessions. When either class is involved with a publishing project, the book buddies will provide an appreciative audience. Since the writing and publishing experience is frequently a component of a wider classroom theme or unit, it is certainly possible to integrate the book buddy program into that theme. Figure 3.4 provides a summary of one book buddy project the authors shared.

(Text continues on page 76.)

TIPS FOR BOOK BUDDY SHARING

1. **Get to know your younger book buddy.** Introduce yourself, tell a little about your interests and hobbies. Ask questions about your buddy's interests too: find out if you have mutual likes or dislikes, especially regarding books.

2. **Bring your favorite books to your first meeting with your book buddy.** If you like these stories and share them enthusiastically, your book buddy will probably enjoy them too. Encourage your buddy to bring a book to share with you next time.

3. **Involve your book buddy.** Try holding the book together. Ask your buddy to help turn the pages and ask questions or to "chime in" when there are repeated or rhyming lines.

4. **Talk about the story.** Discuss the illustrations and how they help tell the story. Invite your buddy to respond to the characters or to predict what might happen next. Encourage your buddy to relate his or her own feelings and experiences, and share your own thoughts too.

5. **Take turns reading.** As you get to know each other better and feel more comfortable about book sharing, you may wish to take turns reading aloud to each other. Be patient if your book buddy stumbles on new words, and don't be afraid to help.

6. **Practice reading your book.** If you feel uncomfortable at first about reading aloud, practice reading your book first. Remember that your younger buddy will not be critical of your reading. You may prefer to tell the story and use the illustrations to assist you. Simply practice telling the story to yourself as you look at the illustrations. Use your voice to bring the characters alive for your buddy.

Fig. 3.2. Tips for Book Buddy Sharing.

SELECTION TIPS FOR BOOK BUDDIES

1. **Begin with your own favorites.** If you have always liked the story, chances are your book buddy will enjoy it too.

2. **Keep the books short.** Try to find books that are not too long. Later on your buddy will probably appreciate longer picture books or chapter books. Take your time to look at the illustrations and determine whether these will appeal to you and your buddy.

3. **Stick to simple stories.** Predictable books, like those by Pat Hutchins or Kathy Stinson, are good choices for younger children. The patterns in these stories are easily found and repeated often and your book buddy will enjoy these story patterns.

4. **Use your buddy's favorite authors.** Your book buddy will be delighted when you introduce new titles by their favorite authors. When you take the time to find these books or any books that appeal to your buddy's interests or to current classroom (or seasonal) themes, you will be rewarded with a happy sharing time.

5. **Talk about your successful book sharing choices with your classmates.** Ask them for recommendations too.

6. **Try writing your own stories and books for your book buddy.** These personalized selections will make you feel proud of your efforts, and they will be appreciated by your buddy. The favor may even be returned and your book buddy may want to share original stories with you.

7. **Select books with your buddy.** Plan to visit the school library with your buddy to select books for sharing. Your teacher may wish to schedule such visits at times when the teacher-librarian is available to assist you. You will be able to demonstrate how to use the card catalogue or computer to search for books.

Fig. 3.3. Selection Tips for Book Buddies.

BOOK BUDDIES IN ACTION

One grade 5 class was involved in a literature-based theme that focused on the novel *The Midnight Fox* by Betsy Byars. The students were also reading several different Byars novels in their literature circles. In addition to these text sets, the classroom teacher chose to read aloud *The Summer of the Swans*, and there were many opportunities for response and discussion about these stories by Betsy Byars.

Then the whole class visited the library resource center, and the teacher-librarian used book-talks to introduce the students to several different books; each book was a story or collection of tales about foxes. Since the students had been working on character studies, the teacher-librarian focused their attention on the fox characters in the books. The students were already divided into literature circles to read their Byars novels, and each group chose one "fox" book to read and discuss together. Some chose picture books; others chose folktales. Longer fiction books were not used in this activity but were included in the booktalks, and students were allowed to sign these out later for independent reading.

At a later session the students reported back to the class and there was a lively discussion about the different ways in which the fox is depicted in literature. Several students indicated that they were reading the fox stories to their grade 1 book buddies and that they have discussed foxes with their younger buddies. This was a good opportunity to introduce the concept of character stereotyping. The classroom teacher told the class that they would each be writing and publishing their own picture book about a fox. Since this was close to the end of the school year, the students decided that these books should be given to their book buddies after their final sharing session. The teacher-librarian and the classroom teacher provided conferencing assistance to the students as they wrote and illustrated their original books. Each contained a dedication to the author's book buddy as well as an "about the author" section, including the author's photograph. The grade 1 recipients were overjoyed with these book gifts, and the final sharing session was a happy time indeed.

When the teacher-librarian and the classroom teacher met to evaluate the theme, they agreed that they had been better able to reach their learning objectives by planning and teaching collaboratively. A high degree of student participation and enjoyment was evident, particularly during the book publishing project for the grade 1 book buddies.

Fig. 3.4. Book Buddies in Action.

Interactive Educational Technologies

Although the human touch is always best, it is also possible to "share the story" using an interactive multimedia approach. The introduction of exciting new educational technologies, such as CD-ROM and hypermedia programs, allows students to become more actively involved. The teacher-librarian plays a new role in helping students incorporate this technology into their daily lives. Commercially prepared CD-ROM programs, such as the National Geographic *Mammals—a Multimedia Encyclopaedia, Incredible Cross-Sections,* Discis Books, and hypermedia programs created by teachers and students are truly interactive. The student reads text and graphics, views still or moving pictures, listens to realistic sounds, and responds individually to the computer program.

It is easy for students to use interactive multimedia programs to enjoy stories or to select and use information from a variety of programs for their own purposes. Students also can use this technology to produce their own original products. These range from simple stories with scanned pictures and digitized sounds to an original multimedia presentation that incorporates many information-processing skills and strategies. This type of presentation is a welcome alternative to the traditional written products, such as reports and essays. Product sharing also takes on a new dimension when students use technology to communicate their thoughts and information in original programs. Audience involvement is guaranteed, and these student-prepared programs may be reused as learning resources in the future.

The school library resource center is rapidly becoming the school's production center as well as the information center with the availability of multimedia workstations, CD-ROM stations, and the computers that are used to search and circulate resources. Access to computer word processors will allow students to create most of their original presentation before adding any desired special features. The teacher-librarian and the classroom teacher who are working cooperatively to develop resource-based learning opportunities for their students will be able to include appropriate educational technology in order to truly develop literacy.

Highlighting and Promoting Writing

The school library resource center program provides many opportunities to promote and to highlight the importance of reading and writing. The teacher-librarian's involvement in literacy promotion will be evident in the library resource center's displays, which are constantly being developed and changed throughout the school year. A seasonal and holiday display center, for example, may provide better access to these popular materials for students and teachers. When seasonal books are in demand, a special circulation arrangement such as "one-day loan" or "library resource center use only," will allow everyone to enjoy them.

Of course it follows that students will need adequate opportunities to visit the school library resource center in order to make the best use of these displays. Otherwise, they will be viewed as decorative rather than accessible. A display of a particular author's books and interesting information about the author may be provided for a class author study or prior to that author's visit to the school. Many students and teachers will then have access to these materials, rather than a few fortunate classrooms or individuals who might have discovered them before everyone else. These special displays are soon received with enthusiasm as teachers and students realize that equal access and opportunities for reading and enjoyment are better assured.

The school library resource center may also be the location for displays of students' writing. Again, with pleasing displays and procedures for using these materials they become available to the entire school. The promotion of reading and writing through the effective involvement of students in the actual processes is an important component of the partnership between the classroom and the school library resource program.

Students as Authors

When classrooms are involved in publishing projects, such as the fox picture books that were written, illustrated, and published within the "Foxes/Byars" theme, the teacher-librarian's involvement is welcomed. The completed books may be shared with their intended audience in the library resource center, and a student book display will promote reading and writing across the school. Many teacher-librarians will suggest an extended display period for books by student authors. After these books have been available for a month, for example, they are then returned to the classroom for further sharing before the student takes the books home. The fox books were first displayed in the library resource center, then enjoyed in the classrooms of the book buddies before they were eventually taken home by the first-grade students. Students who write and publish their own writing within a classroom publishing project experience the satisfaction of being an author, and these opportunities for sharing with others will reinforce this positive experience.

When the teacher-librarian is involved in the writing and publishing process, the concept of the library resource center as a location for creating and sharing is also emphasized. This type of activity is frequently included in the thematic units that are collaboratively planned by classroom teachers and teacher-librarians. Holding a conference with students is an essential part of writing and publishing; revising and editing are time consuming and demanding. Classroom teachers recognize the benefits for their students when the teacher-librarian accepts and welcomes this type of participation.

Mentoring Projects

The "mentor project" is a good example of this type of involvement in the reading/writing process. The mentors may be volunteer parents, university students, senior citizens, or any individuals who enjoy writing and assisting students through the writing and publishing process. In one such project, a yearly Writers' Club attracts many upper elementary students. The teacher-librarian coordinates the after-school project with several classroom teachers and a language arts professor at a local university. When the enthusiastic pre-service teacher education students arrive at the school, they are paired with the students in the Writers' Club. When the demand is great, the university students work with small groups rather than individual students. The enthusiastic elementary students are ready to discuss their ideas for their own books, and the mentors are prepared to meet with them and to offer suggestions throughout the process. The mentor project concludes with a "publishing party"—the finished books are shared at an evening Book Launching, which is attended by delighted parents, teachers, and friends of the young student authors.

Other schools involve students in a language arts fair, which provides a cross-school focus on student reading and writing. Samples of students' writing and publishing are displayed in the school library resource center, and these are read and enjoyed by parents and other special guests. Such special events as the Book Launch are received with as much enthusiasm as the annual school science fair, and they attract local media and authors who enjoy sharing the joy of writing with the young authors.

Author Visits

Students who have experienced the sense of accomplishment that accompanies student authorship have a deeper appreciation for the professional author's work. When an author is invited to visit elementary school students, this activity may be a memorable occasion for everyone. The author may be a local person who writes for children and visits them frequently, or the individual may be a nationally recognized and well-known author. Their visits will be equally anticipated and welcomed by classroom teachers and students. When the teacher-librarian and the classroom teacher are able to incorporate an author's visit into their plans, the necessary preparation for the actual event is more effective and enjoyable for everyone.

Sometimes an entire class or several classes will participate in the author's visit, but it is also possible to select interested students from across the school to meet the author and then share their experience with other students. A display of information about the author, including his or her books, may be centrally located in the library resource center, and these materials will be used by students and teachers prior to the author's visit to the school. Perhaps the display and the author's visit are part of a classroom or grade level's current thematic study. A visit by an author of mystery books, such as Eric Wilson, for example, would provide an exciting culmination for a theme centered around the mystery genre.

The display may serve several purposes in addition to providing access to the author's books. A learning center might be employed where students would use the biographical information to write their own stories about the author. The teacher-librarian will be able to suggest many print and nonprint materials for such a pertinent resource based learning center. The activities that are planned around the center will also involve the teacher-librarian in an instructional as well as a managerial role. Of course, an actual visit from the author is not always feasible, but it is certainly possible to add life and excitement to a theme by meeting the author through a video presentation or the writing of students who have processed information and created their own presentation about the author.

When the author does visit in person, the library resource center is also the perfect location for the meeting. Teacher-librarians are often involved in district, provincial, or state projects that organize school speaking tours for visiting authors. They will be informed about costs and conditions for the school visit. Authors have preferences for audience size and appropriate age groups, and these will be respected by visit-coordinators who wish to accommodate the author and make the meeting as valuable as possible for the students. These efforts will certainly be appreciated by the visiting author.

When students have been properly prepared and exhibit interest and knowledge about the author and their writing, the exchange will be significant. Authors will honestly answer the students' questions about their books and their approach to writing, and the young participants will realize that authors are indeed real people, like themselves, who also encounter occasional problems with their writing. Many schools attempt to provide this special opportunity to promote reading and writing on a regular basis, assuring that all students experience several author visits during their elementary years.

Where student library monitor clubs exist, there will also be opportunities to involve the members in the preparations for the author's visit. Colorful posters will welcome the author, and these students really appreciate informal receptions or lunch with the special guest. What a wonderful way to show appreciation for the monitors' work throughout the school year. Many visiting authors have expressed their pleasure when they are invited to meet these eager young people in addition to the more formal setting of the actual presentation.

Classroom teachers and parents also appreciate this carefully planned attempt to involve more students in a meaningful way in the authors' visits to the school.

Highlighting and Promoting Reading

At the same time that students' writing is being encouraged, many activities can be developed to promote reading. The school library has traditionally operated programs that tried to encourage students to read, but these activities were often developed by the teacher-librarians alone and without any thought to integrating their efforts into classroom activities. With greater emphasis on reading as a lifelong activity and the growing awareness that we must develop readers who not only can read but want to read, classroom teachers and teacher-librarians are working closer together to encourage students to read.

USSR, DEAR, SQUIRT, and WARTS

To become readers, students have to read. Educators must provide in-school time for everyone to read. Effective schools that want to promote reading as the key to lifelong learning have in place a policy for daily silent reading by teachers and students. Whether it's called Uninterrupted Sustained Silent Reading (USSR), Drop Everything And Read (DEAR), Sustained Quiet Uninterrupted Independent Reading Time (SQUIRT), or We All Read Together Silently (WARTS), students need to see that the adults around them are readers and are willing to spend part of their day sitting quietly and reading. Modeling has been described as the significant factor in the success of these silent reading programs (Hart-Hewins and Wells, 1992), and most teachers today give some time for silent reading each day. Figure 3.5 summarizes several tips for successful silent reading programs.

TIPS FOR SUCCESSFUL SILENT READING PROGRAMS

There are several commonly stated agreements about silent reading programs:

a) Use it everyday, no exceptions.

b) Let students choose what they read.

c) Don't use it as part of a reward or punishment system.

d) Use it early in the day and not as a way to "settle" the children after playtime.

e) The teacher must read too!

Fig. 3.5. Tips for Successful Silent Reading Programs.

Reading Day

One way to recognize reading as an integral part of life and to activate the partnership between the classroom and the school library is to set aside a day where nothing but reading happens. Let students pick a theme and develop what things they would like to do. For instance, a Beach Party in January can be lots of fun. Everyone brings in a beach towel, umbrellas, sunglasses, picnic coolers, or sand toys and spends the day at the "beach" with their favorite books. The teacher-librarian (as the lifeguard) could select materials and give booktalks on books related to the beach theme. Then long periods of silent reading, chances to visit each other's towels, breaks for a refreshing snack, and even a swim in the local pool could all be part of the day. Repeating the reading day once a month with different themes could be lots of fun. Groups of classes could get together and even the whole school could be involved in developing different uses for this idea. How about a reading "sleepover"?

Dress-Up Day

A variation of reading day is **dress-up day**, when everyone comes dressed as their favorite character from a fairy tale, characters from a recently shared read aloud, characters from a novel, or a famous person from history. Students could question each other about who they are, find and read books about this person, or have a parade and visit other classes. Teachers could dress up as well, perhaps as mystery characters that could only be found out by reading certain books. At L.M. Montgomery Elementary School, which was named for the author of the Anne of Green Gables novels, the entire school celebrates this beloved author's birthday by dressing up in period costume.

Home Reading Programs

Parents want their children to be readers and they want to be involved in developing their children's interest in reading. Schools are recognizing that they must involve parents and the community in real ways with the school's literacy program. Before their children began school, most parents spent a great deal of time reading to their children and involving them in early literacy events. Educators need to develop ways that allow parents to continue that involvement in their children's literacy development. One way is by developing a **home reading program** in which students and their parents spend some time each evening reading together. Developing a routine at home that matches the silent reading program at school helps students see that reading is not just a school thing. A book could be started at school and then the child could take it home and finish it there. It's not demanded as homework but as a natural extension of what they have been doing in school. Students should be encouraged to bring books from home that they started there and want to finish at school.

Parents and their children should use some system to track the reading that was done at home on a simple reading record sheet, a reading log, or some other technique developed by the student. Perhaps at parent-teacher interview time, parents could bring in their "report card" to share with the teacher—a list of the books read and any observations made by the parents and the child. It's really a matter of building a sense that we have a shared responsibility in this area.

Summer Reading Programs

Another traditional program organized by the school library (and often found in public libraries as well) is the **summer reading program**. Students are invited to join a summer reading club and write down the titles of all items they read over the summer. In September when they return to school, they receive a small reward for taking part. Such programs are welcomed by many parents, particularly parents of younger students, as a way to keep the momentum of school reading habits building over the summer. Care must be taken to ensure that these programs are not perceived as a negative thing by students, who are expecting a long break from school. Such negative feelings are often a symptom that reading has not been developed as a natural thing that is part of our daily lives. It may be a better idea to hook the summer reading program into the already established home reading program that operated throughout the school year. It is then seen as an extension of the home reading program and more a part of the total literacy program.

Book Fairs

Many teacher-librarians regularly schedule at least one **book fair** each year for their school. These are excellent opportunities to highlight the importance of reading by making books available for purchase. When this sort of activity is supported by the school and the community, it is possible to promote reading as well as raise funds for the school library resource center. Many schools organize a group of parents who volunteer their time to assist with the operation of a book fair. Students enjoy browsing through the display of new books, and they experience the joy of selecting, purchasing, and owning their own books. Book buddies sometimes visit the sale together, allowing the older student to assist the younger buddies with their selections and purchases.

Students also enjoy **used-book auctions**, where they bid on donated books. The auctioneer, often the teacher-librarian or, even better, the principal, sets a limit for the bids. Students enjoy this activity immensely. The **book swap** is another promotion that does not involve money; students bring a book donation to the library resource center and exchange with students from other classrooms. It's a good idea to encourage everyone to bring one type of book (for example, paperback books in good condition) to ensure that everyone selects a book of similar quality and value.

Celebrations

Most literacy programs include the concept of celebration as an important part of the process. These are usually culmination events that recognize the achievements of students after an extended period of time working on some topic or theme. They may also serve as opportunities to celebrate the publication of students' works or the performances and productions associated with their language arts activities. It is a valuable opportunity for classroom teachers and the teacher-librarian to activate their partnership.

Poetry Festival

One event that can be used in a variety of ways is to hold a festival. It could take the form of a drama festival, puppetry festival, or a poetry festival. A whole school could spend several weeks focusing on poetry—reading, writing, and sharing poetry. Read alouds, choral readings, recitations, visits to the school by poets, and many writing activities could be held in each classroom. As a grand finale to the festival, a day-long series of events could be planned to share with other classes what has been happening. Parents, grandparents, and local people could be invited for some of the events. Artworks created by the students to go with their poetry could be viewed. Performances of choral readings, individual poems, limericks, and the ever popular "raps" could provide lots of fun, all centered on poetry.

Classroom teachers and the teacher-librarian could work together to facilitate the poetry festival by partnering for art activities, studies of writers, writing activities, rehearsals for presentations, and publishing poetry books. The teacher-librarian could supply lots of books, AV materials, and community resources, as well as giving readings, working with choral groups, and hosting many festival events in the school library resource center.

Science and Language Arts Fairs

Most schools are familiar with science fairs, in which pairs of students prepare a display based on the science research they have completed and share that display with peers and parents at the annual fair. Projects are judged, prizes are awarded, and winners compete at district, state, or provincial competitions that follow. Unfortunately, many of these science fair projects are expected to be completed outside of school time and wind up being completed more or less by parents rather than students. These events then are not the type of celebration we are advocating.

Projects in science should be integrated into a school's science program, where the perusing of scientific investigation is part of the overall instructional program, demonstrated by teachers and emulated by students. With the move to more active, child-centered curriculum, it is no longer acceptable to assign science projects and expect that they be completed at home. When students work on a science project as part of their science program at school, then the Science Fair truly becomes an opportunity to use their communication skills in a real situation and to celebrate their scientific achievements. Classroom teachers and teacher-librarians need to address this issue together with the goal of developing a schoolwide plan for integrating these celebrations into the plan for the science program.

With the whole language philosophy has come a realization that we need to also celebrate the achievements students have made in their language arts. Some schools hold a **Language Arts Fair** (often in the spring) where students from across the school create displays, prepare presentations, and set up exhibits as a way of sharing with their peers and parents some of their best efforts over the year. These fairs are very exciting events that students thrive on. They seem to take right over and surpass even our most optimistic expectations. Events like these make for "real-life" situations in which students have a purpose for the use of oral and visual skills in the sharing of ideas and information. This is the direction we must move if we are to prepare our students for independent lifelong learning.

Birthday Parties for Famous Writers

Children always respond with interest to any information about the lives of the writers who create their favorite books. One way to celebrate these lives is to hold a birthday party for one of their favorites. Information on the birth dates of well-known writers is easy to locate, and a birthday party could easy be planned by students. Because it's impossible to have the person there for the party, the author's books could become the focal point. Rereadings of their books could start the party, followed by the making of a giant birthday card for everyone to sign and mail to the writer. Of course, cake, balloons, and the other traditions of birthday parties would be included. Everyone loves a birthday party!

Theme Celebration

The conclusion of a collaboratively planned thematic unit may be held in the school library resource center. In the typical celebration of learning that culminates the classroom theme, students are involved in sharing their work in interesting ways. When products include publishing or multimedia presentations or models or other displays, everyone is keen to enjoy the results of the learning process. Skills in presentation are developed and appropriate audience participation is encouraged. A "stations" approach may be organized, and other students may be invited to visit each station or center, where individuals or groups of students share their work. This helps involve the audience and prevents the boring parade of one student after another presenting his or her part. It also provides classroom teachers and the teacher-librarian with another opportunity to observe students as they present and discuss their products. Food preparation is often one part of this type of celebration, especially when a particular culture, country, or time period has been studied. Samples of food or a taste of celebration cakes add to the enjoyment and the sense of celebration that are part of this type of concluding event.

Special Weeks

There are many national celebrations that focus on reading, writers, and libraries. **Library Week**, usually held in April, is always an opportunity to coordinate special events among various public, school, and specialty libraries. Students need to learn there are other community-based library services that will offer them information services and recreational reading material long after they leave school. In Canada, **Canadian Children's Book Week** (usually held in November) is of particular importance to school libraries. It is a chance to promote reading and writing on a national scale and in particular to celebrate the many great Canadian writers and illustrators of children's books. Classroom teachers and teacher-librarians have developed many activities that highlight both of these national celebrations. Often teacher-librarians arrange to have author visits within these special weeks because national or district funding is often available to cover some of the costs. There are also commercially available materials, such as posters, bookmarks, bibliographies, and theme-related promotional materials, that can form the basis of the school-based celebration of these events.

Children are often invited to take part in poster contests, designing bookmarks, readings by visiting authors, and other special reading and writing events planned collaboratively by the classroom teacher and the teacher-librarian. Library Week may assume the special flavor of an identified theme, which is captured in a slogan or promotional materials like posters or bookmarks. "Reading Exercises the Brain," for example, encourages everyone to read, and it promotes the exploration of books about physical fitness and sports. Appropriate displays and activities may be collaboratively planned by classroom teachers and the teacher-librarian.

These special literacy activities and celebrations are always most effective when developed to meet the shared goals of the classroom theme or unit and the school library resource center program. They are less effective if developed and offered solely by the teacher-librarian in isolation from the rest of the school's curriculum. When the responsibility for advocating and developing literacy is shared by the educational partners, everyone will benefit from the resulting dynamic literacy program. Classroom teachers are better able to meet the learning objectives for their students, and the teacher-librarian will be better able to lead the integration of literacy and information skills and strategies across the school's curriculum. As students interact with appropriate learning resources and are actively involved in carefully planned activities, they truly become independent learners whose literacy skills will continue to develop throughout their lives.

RESOURCE-BASED UNITS OF STUDY

The third major area where the classroom teacher and the teacher-librarian may activate their partnership is in the developing, teaching, and evaluating of resource-based units of study (RBUs). The following RBUs are examples of resource-based learning in action and were developed by classroom teachers and a teacher-librarian using the collaborative planning process. Topics were generated by student interests and the school's curriculum. All of the RBUs described here were developed using a similar planning process, were repeated with several classes of children, and were recorded by the teacher-librarians involved. The planning guides were retained by the teacher-librarian and were used successfully in subsequent years after necessary revisions were made.

When classroom teachers and teacher-librarians activate their partnership for resource-based learning they do so to develop three types of RBUs—literary RBUs that focus on literature; content-area RBUs in subjects like social studies, health, and science; and thematic RBUs that integrate all or several areas of the curriculum. The following RBUs developed in our two schools provide examples of each type.

Literary Unit: MEDIEVAL LIFE

Background

The Middle Ages is a time period that has great appeal for sixth-grade students. Excellent learning materials are abundant, including print, nonprint, and human resources. By planning and working together, the classroom teacher, teacher-librarian, and students will engage in a richly satisfying resource-based learning opportunity.

This theme began as a class novel study on *A Door in the Wall* by Newbery Award-winning author Marguerite de Angeli. With time, and with the input of several teachers and their classes, it has grown and developed into a literature-based theme that incorporates several curriculum areas. The teacher-librarian provided resources for the literature study of historical fiction, presented information on the genre itself, took part in literature circle discussions that centered on historical fiction, and shared in several literature response activities. Many worthwhile activities developed to meet the shared goals of the educational partners. Some of these took place in the school library, and responsibility for instruction and evaluation was shared. The interest on the part of students in this topic was quite high, and it was recognized as an excellent opportunity for activating the information process. The classroom was decorated to become medieval "castles," with mural paper painted to resemble stone and tissue paper "stained glass" windows.

The unit overview provided here is really a focus on how students used the information process to extend their literature study and write reports on one aspect of medieval life. The whole theme was brought to a close with a great medieval feast that included the sharing of these reports.

The teacher-librarian's involvement in the medieval life theme has grown with the development of the theme itself. Planning has always been important, and classroom teachers and the teacher-librarian continue to make revisions to accommodate each new group of students. As curriculum varies and new resources are located, objectives, activities, and evaluation methods may change. The teacher-librarian has always been most actively involved in instruction and evaluation in these areas:

1. promotion and appreciation of the literature genres, historical fiction, epics, and legends (traditional literature);

2. guiding students as they engage in the information process.

This second area of involvement, with information processing, will be described in some depth in this outline.

Goals

Students will have an opportunity to choose one aspect of life in medieval times that is of particular interest to them. By interacting with various types of information the students will be able to answer their own questions in a meaningful way.

Objectives

Students will:

1. develop their understanding of the information process by using it to learn about medieval life;

2. develop and use questions that will guide their inquiry;

3. select and use information that is relevant for their own needs (to answer their questions);

4. develop an understanding of how their own questions may be used to organize the information they gather; and

5. organize and present their findings in a report.

Since the introduction of the information processing activity several years ago, the teachers have developed an alternate approach that is frequently used. If students have already written a major report during the sixth grade, they work within interest groups to activate the information process and create a product of their choice that will be presented to and evaluated by their classmates and teachers. A partial list of some possible products and useful evaluation strategies have been included in appendix C.

Resources

Special resources for the theme are stored in a theme box in the school library. Many others were available from the regular collection in the school library or borrowed from the general collection and from other school or public libraries.

The medieval life theme box includes a wide variety of print and nonprint resources, such as videotapes of presentations by local resource persons or student projects, calligraphy instructions, and articles about legends and heraldry. The human resources used included the children's librarian from the local public library, who gave a presentation entitled "Robin Hood and Life in the Middle Ages"; the school's music teacher, who gave a class on Christmas carols and recorder and autoharp music; students from the Junior High School, who gave flute demonstrations; a local expert who gave an archery demonstration; and a retired university professor, who spoke about medieval times and the importance of legends in literature.

Information Skills

The following information skills have been taken from the Information Skills Continuum (Province of Prince Edward Island Department of Education, 1990) and are organized into the stages within the information process. These will require instruction, reinforcement, or review.

1. Planning Stage
   - choose appropriate materials for a specified topic
   - develop individual questions to guide inquiry

2. Gathering Information
   - distinguish between relevant and irrelevant information

3. Interacting with Information
   - make concise notes from various types of resources

4. Organizing Information
   • write a simple outline (or use individual questions) to organize information

5. Creating Information
   • write a content-related report that includes a title page, a table of contents, and a bibliography
   • compile a simple bibliography

6. Presenting Information
   • share reports and personal products with classmates, teachers, and parents

7. Evaluating the Process
   • use established criteria to evaluate peers presentations
   • evaluation of written and oral products by teacher-librarian and classroom teacher

Classroom Teacher's Role

1. Facilitate the initial brainstorming session. Record the information (key words, facts, ideas) students already have acquired through classroom activities or independent reading while resources were available in the classroom and the various novels were read and discussed.

2. Outline for students the expectations for the information-processing activity. Describe the type of report that will be completed. If possible, show an example of a student's report from a previous year.

3. Assist the teacher-librarian as students develop their own question webs. Meet with individual students to ensure they are prepared to move from the planning stage to the information gathering and interacting stages.

4. Provide students with adequate time to select and interact with learning resources. Use of library passes for individual students or prearranged times for groups of students should be encouraged to ensure adequate accessibility to resources for all students.

5. Check that students are recording appropriate information in concise, point-form notes on fact sheets.

6. Assist the teacher-librarian with teaching, reinforcing the skill of organizing their information according to their own questions (categorizing and sequencing).

7. Hold a conference with the students (with the assistance of the teacher-librarian) as they draft, revise, and edit their reports.

8. Evaluate the students as they progress through the information process. The teacher-librarian will also provide notes and observations.

9. Evaluate the completed reports, and involve students by allowing them to take part in self-evaluation. Assign the assessment code (e.g., VG = very good) and written comments according to predetermined criteria. (See appendix A for a sample evaluation form for written reports that we have used.)

Teacher-Librarian's Role

Note: Students should have had access to a variety of resources in their classroom before this activity begins.

1. Collect and organize print and nonprint learning resources for the medieval life information center to be located in the library resource center.

2. Provide an overview of the information process; remind students of earlier opportunities for involvement with the process. Stress the importance of using it when approaching a topic as wide and multidimensional as living in the Middle Ages.

3. Assist the teachers with the brainstorming session to establish the students' prior knowledge of medieval life.

4. Teach students how to develop a question web based on one aspect of medieval life that is of particular interest for the individual student. Provide direction and assistance as students develop their webs.

5. Act as a facilitator as students choose resources (from the information center) to answer their questions. Reinforce good searching techniques (e.g., use of a table of contents, use of an index, skimming text, etc.).

6. Review note-taking skills and encourage students to take notes in point form on the fact sheets provided.

7. Teach students how to use their original questions as categories when they organize their information.

8. Assist the teachers when they meet with students as they draft, revise, and edit their reports.

9. Teach simple bibliography skills. These should be developed gradually from primary to upper elementary grades.

10. Assist with evaluation by keeping a checklist or observations about students on paper or on disc at each stage of the information process.

11. Display the students' reports in the library resource center. Provide opportunities for these to be shared with other students (formally or informally).

Students' Role

Note: Ideally, students will have had opportunities to engage in the information process at each grade level since beginning elementary school.

Prior to this formal emphasis on the information process (within the sixth-grade medieval life theme) students will already have been learning a great deal about medieval life in classroom activities as they:

1. read, listen to, and discuss the class novel *The Door in the Wall* (de Angeli);

2. read, discuss, respond to other historical novels (or legends) in their literature circles:

   The Whipping Boy (Fleischman)
   The Little Princes (Melady)

The Sword in the Tree (Bulla)

Minstrel in the Tower (Skurzynski)

Adam of the Road (Gray)

Robin Hood stories (Pyle, Disney, other versions), etc.

3.   Listen to, discuss, and respond to several books that are read aloud by the classroom teacher

Medieval Feast (Aliki)

Castle in the Attic (Winthrop)

Max and Me and the Time Machine (Greer)

Saint George and the Dragon (Hodges)

Sir Gawain and the Loathly Lady (Hastings)

Merry Ever After (Lasker)

4.   Read, view a wide variety of nonfiction books and other nonprint resources about life in the Middle Ages that are available in the classroom for a minimum of one week before they are returned to the library resource center for the medieval life information center. (See the partial list of resources for suggested titles.)

5.   Contribute to a brainstorming session where this new information can be shared with the class.

6.   Choose one aspect of medieval life that is of particular interest to them.

7.   Activate the information process, be able to identify the stages, and to be aware of the skills that are important within these stages.

8.   Take responsibility for preparing a complete report (on one aspect of life in the Middle Ages) and present their work to the teacher and teacher-librarian at each of the identified checkpoints for conferencing and evaluation.
     a. question webs
     b. notes
     c. information organized by categories
     d. rough draft
     e. completed report

9.   Participate in evaluating the process and the product by
     a. writing about each stage of the information process in a response log and
     b. providing their own written comment and letter grade for the completed report

Schedule and Activities

The medieval life theme usually lasts about six weeks (or a little longer if it extends into the Christmas season.) When castle "building" or a concluding celebration occurs, more time will be required.

The teacher-librarian will have opportunities for involvement early in the theme as the genre of historical fiction is introduced along with the novel study. This introduction may require an instructional session with the class, or the students may need assistance with developing their own book reports or book talks. Another connection at that time may occur if the teacher decides to emphasize traditional oral literature, such as legends or ballads. The students may be reading about Robin Hood or King Arthur as they produce their own skits or puppet plays or, as storytellers, they tell or sing about these legendary characters. If a book writing project is planned, the teacher-librarian and the classroom teacher will guide the students as they learn about the manuscripts produced by the monks of long ago. Calligraphy and illumination are of great interest to sixth-grade authors.

The actual information-processing component of this theme requires about three six-day cycles (eighteen school days), which will be a time of intensive involvement with the school library program and the teacher-librarian. It may be practical to schedule this information-processing activity during the second half of the theme, after the language arts and other curricular activities are progressing.

CYCLE ONE

Day One: Introductory Lesson
Location: Classroom or library resource center

The classroom teacher facilitates the brainstorming session (using the chalkboard to record responses). The teacher-librarian assists by categorizing the information into subtopics (e.g., PLACES: castles, cathedrals, monasteries; or PEOPLE: knights, monks, nobility, peasants). Note: A chart or overhead projector will be useful. (See chapter 2 examples.)

Day Two
Location: Library resource center

Teacher-librarian introduces the medieval life information center to the class, then demonstrates the creation of a question web. This web should incorporate one of the subtopics that was identified the day before. The questions "who? what? where? when? why? how?" will be useful in developing questions. Students choose one subtopic (major category of interest) and begin to develop their own questions. (See chapter 2 examples.)

> Checkpoint One: Students must have question webs checked and signed by a teacher or teacher-librarian before proceeding to the next stage.

Note: Copies of the students' question webs may be displayed near the information center in the library resource center for quick reference. Preferably, students will retain their question webs and all other organizers (note-taking sheets, bibliography guides, etc.) in individual theme binders.

Day Three

The teacher outlines for students the expectations for (which are also the criteria for evaluating) the completed reports. The teacher-librarian reviews the rules for accessing and using the materials in the medieval life information center and other sources of information (e.g., encyclopedias, periodicals).

Days Four, Five, and Six

Students visit the library resource center in groups. The teacher-librarian provides guidance as students select appropriate resources and assess them (in terms of content organization, readability, and relevant information.)

Cycle Two

Day One
Location: Classroom or library resource center
>The teacher-librarian reviews note-taking skills with the class.

Days Two to Six
>Students will interact with (read, listen, view, discuss) information of various types and take notes on fact sheets. The teacher-librarian will meet with individual students, make observations, and take notes about their work at this crucial stage. For example, the teacher-librarian may want to answer the following questions: Do they work independently? Do they cooperate with others (share resources, give advice, discuss thoughts and opinions)? Do they record relevant information in concise, point-form notes, which will help them answer their own questions? Do they resist copying information from their sources? Do they keep track of their sources for their bibliography? (See appendix B for a "Bibliography Sheet" and a "Bibliography Guide" used in this and other units.)

>Checkpoint Two: All students present their completed notes for a teacher or teacher-librarian to check and sign before proceeding to the next stage.

Cycle Three

Days One and Two
>Students should be ready to begin organizing their information. The teacher-librarian and teacher assess how many students have completed Checkpoint Two; if everyone has reached this stage, the teacher-librarian prepares to meet with the whole class. If more time is needed by some of the students, the teacher-librarian prepares to meet with those who are ready while the teacher continues checking notes for the others.

Day Two (and/or Three)
Location: Library resource center
>The teacher-librarian demonstrates how students' own questions, from their webs, can be used to make categories for organizing information. This is best done by using a student's actual question web and fact sheet and an overhead projector. Sometimes a question is not fully explored or answered because of insufficient information. Sometimes the questions are too limiting, or in the course of researching students have formulated better questions or key words that can now be used for organizing the information. It is also important to encourage students to share their feelings about this stage in the information process. Organizing information requires a great deal of flexibility and willingness to accept assistance. Response log entries should reflect the students' reactions.

>Several strategies could be used for the actual organizing of the facts. Students could color code individual facts according to the category in which they fall. A numbering system could also be used in which students assign a number to each category and then put the number for each fact in front of it. For primary students and students with special needs, the fact sheets

could be cut up and then the individual facts sorted into categories. The slips of paper could then be glued onto sheets and the category could be named. Any system that clearly demonstrates to students the organizing process could be employed. Students are also very creative in inventing their own systems. (See appendix B for a sample form used to assist students in categorizing their notes.)

> Checkpoint Three: Teacher and teacher-librarian will meet with each student and check and initial their work. The students should have their facts organized by categories. The teacher and teacher-librarian may want students to indicate an acceptable sequence for these categories (by numbering them) before they attempt their first draft.

Days Four, Five, and Six
Location: Classroom and library resource center
Students begin to write their first drafts. The teacher and teacher-librarian will meet with individual students as they make revisions and, later, edit their writing.

> Checkpoint Four: Students must have their drafts checked and initialed by a teacher or teacher-librarian before beginning their final copy of their reports.

Cycle Four

As students finish writing and illustrating their reports on medieval life, they should be able to refer back to their teacher's expectations for the finished product. Some students will require assistance with organizing their bibliography; others will simply use the chart that should be available in both the library and the classroom. Criteria (product expectations) may also be available in a chart that is either displayed or given to students as a handout. These might include the following:

a cover (required information)

a title page (required information)

a table of contents

underlined headings

an introduction or a conclusion, or both

colored, labeled illustrations, diagrams, etc.

edited writing (correct spelling, punctuation, grammar)

a glossary

neatness

acceptable length

a bibliography

Students should be given time to write a paragraph about their reports. They should also refer to the list of criteria for the product and to their response logs for their feelings about the information-processing experience. They may also be asked to suggest a letter grade for the report, which they feel is warranted.

When students are involved in self-evaluation and this information is used and provided for parents (when reports are sent home to be signed or they are discussed at conference time) teachers' final evaluations are more readily accepted and viewed as being "fair." Teacher-librarian's notes, and observations will also be welcome when evaluations are written. Teachers will want to retain copies of students' reports for their portfolios or for future theme work. However, it is also important to ensure that students have opportunities to share these with other students (by either presenting them to groups of other students or displaying them in the library resource center).

Results

The reports on medieval life will be one important aspect of the celebration that takes place as this theme concludes. A display may form the setting for a musical or dramatic sharing session. Teachers may wish students to present some of the writing or artwork they have produced during the theme. Perhaps the celebration will happen in the "castle," and the teacher-librarian will be invited as a "feast" is shared and games are played.

Students who have had the opportunity to engage in a collaboratively planned, taught, and evaluated activity, such as this medieval life activity, will benefit in many ways. Not only will they learn a great deal about life in an earlier time, they will gain valuable experience in processing information. This resource-based learning opportunity requires commitment from each of the educational partners, and success is inevitable for those who are willing to participate in a collaborative spirit. Students will be better equipped to handle information and to use it for their own purposes in the future. The literature that is read by the students in their classrooms will now have a meaningful context, and their ability to relate the stories (and the important themes) to their own contemporary world will be enhanced immeasurably.

Literary Unit:
Author Study • ROBERT MUNSCH

Background

One of the most common literary events in most elementary classrooms is the author study. It is seen as a time to focus on the person behind the books by finding biographical information about the author, trying to understand how they do what they do, and generally trying to demystify writers and the writing process. An author study can give young readers and writers a sense of themselves as authors who are trying to share their feelings, ideas, and experiences with an audience. Any grade level can conduct an author study, and after a few experiences with them, students look themselves for information on the author of the books they are reading.

Earlier in chapter 2, a guide for completing an author study was given as an example of one way to formally introduce students to the information process. It was intended for fourth-, fifth-, or sixth-grade students, who seem more able to focus their attention on the information process itself and develop a metacognitive awareness of what goes on during the information process. This unit on Robert Munsch was completed by third-grade students who had done informal studies of authors before but had never tried to use more formal information-seeking strategies.

The classroom teachers had two general areas they wanted to include in the unit. They wanted to start small group discussions with their children and to center those discussions around literature. During the planning sessions that followed with the teacher-librarian both of these goals, plus the inclusion of some direct instruction on the components of the information process, were integrated into a resource-based unit on Robert Munsch, whom the children had identified as one of their favorite authors.

Goals

Students will read several Robert Munsch books and respond to that reading with small group discussions about his writing. Students will work as a whole class and in small groups to collect information on Robert Munsch and write a class report on him.

Objectives

Students will:

1. self-select and read independently several Robert Munsch books;

2. choose a group to work with and discuss questions on the Munsch books;

3. keep a reading record of the titles read and make a brief written response to either their reading of the books or their group discussion;

4. develop their understanding that the search for information on an author involves a process with specific strategies for implementation; and

5. engage in several whole-class and small-group activities to collect information and write a report on Robert Munsch.

Resources

Seven sets of Robert Munsch books were put together for this study. Each set consisted of five copies of the identical title. The books used were the familiar "mini" editions of the most popular Munsch titles. Also, two or three copies of all his books were taken from the school library resource center collection, the classroom teacher's collection, and from the children's home libraries. Big book editions were used as read-alouds and then set up in the Robert Munsch reading corner in the back of the class.

Several cassette tapes of Munsch telling his stories were also used, as was a *Meet the Author* (Mead, 1987) audio-visual kit. This kit was used as the main source of information on the author. Several posters of Munsch and his books were also part of an attractive display in the classroom.

Information Skills

The following information skills were identified as ones to be taught in this unit:

1. Record information from various sources.

2. Exchange ideas through discussion.

3. Find specific information using pictures and filmstrips.

4. Identify components of fiction (e.g., author's style, use of words).

5. Develop techniques to record and organize information.

Classroom Teacher's Role

The classroom teacher worked closely with the teacher-librarian, collaborating in many of the activities described above. In particular, the classroom teacher was responsible for:

1. facilitating students' discussion skills;

2. assisting in the formation of the discussion groups;

3. developing questions for the groups to discuss;

4. providing daily silent reading, group discussion time, and time for response in their reading record booklet;

5. facilitating the information-gathering activity and assisting in the whole-class charting of the group biography;

6. sharing in reading aloud, shared readings, and listening to tapes; and

7. observing students' discussion sessions and providing feedback to them.

Teacher-Librarian's Role

The unit was planned and taught jointly by the classroom teacher and the teacher-librarian. It is described here with one class, but the whole unit was adapted and repeated with another class of third-grade students later. The teacher-librarian was responsible for:

1. launching the project by reading aloud Robert Munsch's *Show and Tell*;

2. working with the classroom teacher to coordinate the discussions held by each small group;

3. introducing and helping students fill out their first entry in the "Marvellous Munsch Booklet," which was prepared by the teacher-librarian for each student as a recording device to keep track of books they had read;

4. introducing the concepts associated with the process-oriented approach to information seeking;

5. guiding the completion of a whole-class writing of a short "biography" of Robert Munsch;

6. facilitating the enjoyment of Munsch books by taking part in shared readings of big books, listening to Munsch tell stories on tape, and helping model silent reading of his books; and

7. observing students' discussion behaviors and providing feedback to them.

Students' Role

Students were keenly interested in Robert Munsch and seemed genuinely excited to have their teacher and the teacher-librarian working together. They were expected to:

1. read several Munsch books independently;

2. record the books they read and respond to their reading and their group discussions;

3. engage actively in the group discussions and whole-class lessons; and

4. work collaboratively within their discussion group.

Schedule and Activities

This resource-based unit was designed to be completed on a daily basis over a two-week period. It was felt that the daily silent reading, the group interactions, and the follow-up activities would help to maintain the strong initial interest. The daily schedule also helped in giving the overview of the information process because students were able to complete the whole project within this time. All activities were carried out in the classroom.

Day One

The previous day the classroom teacher and the students had designed the small groups and arranged the classroom with tables gathered together in groups of four. On the first day of the Munsch unit, the teacher-librarian came into the class to introduce the new Munsch book, read it aloud, and open things up for a whole-group discussion. The class discussed how discussions were done, why they were done, and what some of the rules were for successful discussions. The classroom teacher charted these for everyone to see.

Students were then given a set of four identical books by Munsch and invited to read silently. The two teachers read too. After about 15 minutes of reading, students met in their groups to discuss what they had read. Each group was given a question that they could use to get things going if they couldn't think of anything to discuss. The teachers visited the groups, listening and facilitating when appropriate. After a few minutes, the whole class listened as brief reports of the discussions were shared.

The teacher-librarian then introduced the "Marvelous Munsch Booklets," in which the students recorded the book information on the title they had read and wrote any response they wished. The Robert Munsch center was then set up by the children in a reading corner in the class.

Day Two

The teacher-librarian led a shared reading of the big book version of *Mud Puddle* by Robert Munsch. At the end a whole-class discussion focused on the similarities between this book and the title from yesterday. A silent reading time was held like the first day, then a group discussion, a whole-class feedback, and then writing in the response booklets.

Days Three, Four, and Five

The classroom teacher and the students continued with the basic format of the first two days, reading, writing, and talking about Munsch books.

Day Six

The teacher-librarian returned to begin the information-process activity. A general overview of the process was given, and it was noted that the first step of "preparing for the information process" was something we had already started. To tap into prior knowledge, students discussed what they knew about Munsch already. They recorded these "facts," and the groups reported to the whole class. These "facts" were charted as a whole class on large sheets of chart paper that were lined and made to look like a fact sheet. A discussion was held on other sources of information on Munsch, and we made a list of these, including telephoning him, writing him a letter, reading the backs of his books, talking to someone who knew him, etc.

The classroom teacher set up the audio-visual presentation for all to view. This *Meet the Author* kit gives a great deal of information on Robert Munsch, including biographical facts and how he writes his books. After viewing, the discussion groups met and recorded facts.

A whole-class sharing resulted in several charts being filled with facts on Munsch. Students were then shown the original chart that outlined the information process for them and shown how they had moved from the first stage of preparing through the gathering stage into the interacting with the information stage of the information process.

Day Seven

The teacher-librarian quickly pointed out where the students were in the process and discussed the next stage: organizing the information. Together, the class read over the large fact sheets and tried to identify facts they thought went together. These were color coded, so, for example, things that told about Munsch as a child were marked with a yellow check mark, things that told about his books were red, and so on through all the facts. The students decided on the major categories and debated which items went where. At the end there were several facts that didn't seem to go anywhere.

When all the facts were sorted, the large chart sheets were given to the students and they cut them up. All facts were then grouped by color and glued onto a large brown sheet. When all the grouping was done, the name for each category was printed above the group. The organizing of the facts was done. This was a very hands-on methodology that allowed students to "see" what happens to facts when we categorize them or put them together for some reason. With older students, facts are collected on personal fact sheets and then sorted on another sheet as part of this stage in the information process. (See appendix H.) Students having difficulty understanding the concepts associated with organizing information can always be shown this very physical way of sorting facts.

Day Eight

Students were led in a group writing of a short biography of Robert Munsch. The organized notes from the day before were used as a guide in this process. Students helped decide which category we should start with; they prioritized the facts in each category; and they suggested ways to join facts into single or compound sentences. This writing process was activated by the classroom teacher and the teacher-librarian in much the same way as any group-story charting might be done. Everyone enjoyed seeing the report take shape, and when we finished the first draft there were lots of suggestions to revise and edit the text. A great cheer went up when we finished the final shared reading of our biography of Robert Munsch.

Day Nine

Students finalized their responses in their reading booklets. They held group discussions on all the Munsch books and listed some of the common characteristics of his stories. They spent time independently reading his books.

Day Ten

This day was set aside as a day for celebration. The teacher-librarian discussed the importance of sharing the information they had found on Munsch. On the computer the teacher-librarian had transcribed their report and made large copies for display and an individual copy for everyone. This was greeted with much excitement. Students then spent the rest of the morning in an art activity focused on exploring the watercolor medium used in many of the illustrations in Munsch's books. A sharing time was held late in the morning during which students shared their reading booklets and paintings.

By way of evaluation, students discussed the project in their small groups and listed what they felt they had learned. They also listed ways to make it better and suggested what they would like to see happen next. The classroom teacher and teacher-librarian had met several times throughout the project to share observations, and these were shared several times with the students throughout the unit. A final sharing of that feedback came on the last session as well.

Results

This project was one of the first experiences for these third-grade teachers with the concepts of cooperative learning and resource-based learning. It went very well and everyone reported having learned a lot. The collaboration between the classroom and the school library resource center was singled out as one very strong aspect. Students liked the choices they were given, the consistent daily effort put into the project, and the opportunity to work with two teachers. The group discussions were slow to get started, but this project formed the foundation for future growth.

This project was ideal for a fall project in third grade because students still love Munsch and are quite capable of reading his books on their own. There are also lots of readily available materials. Later in third grade, there is more interest in novels, so students may not respond as well. It was an ideal way to formally introduce the information process because the writing of a biography has a fairly consistent format. This proved true when later in the year these same students became involved in resource-based units on animals. The whole process was activated again, and students seemed to have in place a mental framework from which to work. They didn't remember everything about the process, but they knew that there was a process involved and that they had to follow it if they were going to be successful.

Content-Area Unit:
AMAZING ANIMALS

Background

One of the common misunderstandings about resource-based learning is that it is really only meant for intermediate-level students and that primary children would find it too difficult. All children respond positively to active learning experiences that give them choice and input into the activities. They thrive on independence and with the guidance of their teachers work well in any resource-based learning environment.

This science unit was used with second-grade students about midway through the year. One of their favorite interest areas is animals, and classroom teachers had involved them in a major integrated theme on animals that incorporated language arts, music, art, mathematics, and science. During this theme, teachers activated the partnership with the teacher-librarian to develop a resource-based unit that allowed students to work independently exploring information on animals.

It is common in animal studies to focus on the same animals over and over again. For instance, we chose deer, rabbits, beaver, and foxes rather than scorpions, snakes, manatees, or others that are not "cute" or "cuddly." This strategy seems repeated as students move through the grades; they learn a lot but it's about the same animals. They need to be encouraged to learn about a wider range of animals so they will develop an appreciation for all animals and their place in the balance of nature. This unit took direct aim at this concern by presenting children with a choice of animals taken from a list of lesser known animals in the series *Amazing Worlds* published by Stoddart. Students then completed a series of independent activities to collect information on some of these animals. (See appendix D for the "Amazing Animals Booklet.")

This project was developed by two second-grade classroom teachers and the teacher-librarian and was completed over a two-week period. Groups of students came for forty-five minutes each day to work independently collecting information on the animals in at least three of the groups. The teacher-librarian provided the initial introduction and stayed for the first and second sessions. After that students came and went from the center independently, calling on the teacher-librarian whenever they had a problem. The other students that were in the classroom worked on other theme-related topics with the classroom teacher. The groups switched back and forth until the activities were completed.

Goals

The overall goal for this RBU was to provide second-grade students with an independent-learning activity on animals. Promoting an understanding of a wider range of animal species was a secondary goal.

Objectives

Students will:

1. develop an appreciation for the more exotic and less familiar animals of the world;

2. develop an understanding of what learning centers are and how they work;

3. complete a fact-gathering activity on at least three of the seven animal group available; and

4. work independently in a multistation learning center.

Resources

The teacher-librarian showed the students several books from the *Amazing Animals* series and seven titles were chosen. The animals decided on by the children included *Amazing Spiders*, *Amazing Poisonous Animals*, *Amazing Monkeys*, *Amazing Fish*, *Amazing Cats*, *Amazing Birds*, and *Amazing Lizards*. Two copies of each book were then used as the resource for students to use in an independent-learning center built in the school library resource center There were seven learning stations set up in the learning center. Each station was marked with a sign for the "amazing animal" of that station. Work space and two chairs were also put in each station. A table was set up in the learning center to store pencils, erasers, markers, crayons and the booklets containing the activities for each student to complete.

Information Skills

The following information skills were taught during this unit of study:

1. Use picture clues to aid in understanding information.

2. Identify a book's author, title, publisher, and year of publication.

3. Record and summarize information gained from various sources, e.g., pictures captions, and charts.

4. Use a book's table of contents.

5. Find specific information within a book.

Classroom Teacher's Role

While groups of students were out of the classroom working in the learning center, the others were instructed by their teachers in related activities on the animal theme. The following were the responsibilities assumed by the classroom teacher:

1. to divide the students into working groups;

2. to help design (in partnership with the teacher-librarian) the advanced organizer to be used by the students in the Amazing Animals center;

3. to teach the use of webs as fact-gathering devices;

4. to reinforce the use of bibliographic information;

5. to monitor students' responses to working independently in the learning center.

Teacher-Librarian's Role

During the planning sessions, it was decided that the teacher-librarian would have the following responsibilities:

1. to build the Amazing Animals learning center in the school library resource center and have within it seven learning stations, each labeled by the title of the book used, such as *Amazing Lizards* and *Amazing Birds*;

2. to introduce the learning center to students and outline the procedures they are to follow;

3. to monitor their work times in the learning center, by guiding their initial sessions and providing any needed support after they are comfortable with the situation;

4. to reinforce the use of fact-gathering webs as a way of saving any information found on their chosen animals;

5. to track their learning with written observations and check work in their "Amazing Animals Booklet," which was designed as an advanced organizer for their visits to the learning center;

6. to teach the use of fact-gathering webs and reinforce gathering bibliographic information on a book, particularly the name of the author, the title, the publisher, and the publication date.

Students' Role

Students were very excited about working outside their classroom on such an independent activity. They enjoyed working with a partner of their choice and then being able to choose which animals to study.

They were expected to do the following:

1. to develop an understanding of how learning centers operate;

2. to work with their partner to complete webs on three animals and fill in the required bibliographic information on the books they used;

3. to manage the learning center procedures and leave their learning stations ready for the next students to use;

4. to monitor their progress by checking off activities as they were completed.

Schedule and Activities

Two 45-minute periods were set aside each day for these students to complete their work. Four groups rotated through the time periods so that each had time in the classroom and then in the learning center.

Day One

Each group made a visit to the learning center, and the teacher-librarian discussed with them the concept of learning centers—that they are often made up of several learning stations organized around the same general topic but with different specific activities. Students were introduced to the "Amazing Animals Booklet" and asked to fill in part of it. The rest of the session was spent exploring the *Amazing Animals* books to be used as the main source of information. This activity really built a lot of excitement about the project.

Back in the classroom, the teachers introduced webs and how to use them as fact-gathering devices.

Day Two

Each group came again to the learning center with the purpose of reviewing how the webs were to be done. Then students were free to pick their partner and then choose their first learning station. The teacher-librarian began helping students access the bibliographic information on their first book and start gathering the facts about these animals.

The web was structured so students had to first choose four animals mentioned in the *Amazing Animals* book they were reading. So, for example, in the book *Amazing Birds* a student may have chosen swans, pelicans, flamingos, and penguins to include in the web. They were then expected to find two facts (more if they wanted) about each group and put them in their web.

Days Three to Seven

Students continued to rotate through the stations and complete their webs. Some moved quickly and others needed more support. Everyone was able to complete two stations, but the vast majority did three. The goals were not to get as much done as possible but to develop skills working on their own to collect the information and to record it to the best of their ability.

Day Eight

This day was for a final visit to finish up and provide feedback on the experience. The "Amazing Animals Booklets" were given back to take home.

Results

Students were very excited by this project. The general feeling was expressed by asking when they could do more similar activities. They commented positively on being able to work in another part of the school and with a different teacher. They liked picking the stations they could go to and being able to read and explore the books they wanted but only having to record facts that were of interest to them.

Both the classroom teachers and the teacher-librarian were also enthusiastic about this RBU. Students really responded positively to the books, and teachers were keen to explore other ways to use this valuable resource. Having students work on the concepts involved and not being too fussy about what content they choose was also seen as a valuable methodology. All of the teachers wanted to see this type of activity grow so it would be incorporated into their repertoire as primary teachers.

Content-Area Unit: Science • FLIGHT

Background

Upper elementary school-aged children (fifth or sixth grade) are fascinated by the scientific principles involved in flight. Many of their science fair projects reflect this interest as they test these principles and their own ideas about flying. Because the science curriculum at these grade levels usually includes a unit on flight or aviation, teachers and teacher-librarians will find natural opportunities to "connect" with their students' interest.

This flight theme developed beyond a classroom science unit as teachers realized how excited their students were when an activity-based approach was used. In addition to the daily experiments with balloons, paper airplanes, and kites, the students displayed a keen interest in those pioneers who invented and perfected flying machines throughout history. They also realized the significance of important principles in these scientific inventions and in their own life experiences. They were motivated to read more about flight pioneers and their quest to unlock the mysteries surrounding the ability to fly.

The novel *The Twenty-One Balloons* was selected for a classroom novel study, and several biographical novels and picture books were used successfully for both literature circle reading and information processing. For example, *Lost Star,* one of several books about Amelia Earhart, can be read and enjoyed as a novel, as well as providing information for the groups' information-processing activity. Their completed large "photo memory poster," a beautifully illustrated product, was evidence of their knowledge and interest in their pioneers' contributions. In addition to the biographical novels, the groups used resources in other formats, which were later gathered into an interesting "Pioneers of Flight" information center in the library resource center. It is suggested that the information-processing activity begin when the groups have finished their literature circle reading and discussion. This is also a good time for the teacher to devote more classroom time to the science experiments in the unit while continuing to read aloud the novel and recommended picture books.

A trip to the local airport, including a tour of an airplane, and a "mini air show," in which students demonstrated their own flying machines, were exciting concluding events. The flight theme has become a favorite with students. It provides good opportunities for cooperative, active learning with emphasis on the scientific, information, and creative processes. The students' individual and group products should reveal successful learning outcomes in the form of new scientific and biographical knowledge and positive attitudes towards the pioneering spirit and achievements of others.

Goals

Students will learn about important scientific principles involved in flight:

1. Floating, gliding, powered flying are types of flight.

2. Heat creates updrafts of air.

3. How fast an object falls is related to its mass and shape.

4. Moving air can move objects.

5. Drag is a force that slows falling objects.

6. Thrust is a force that can push objects forward.

7. Air moving across a wing-shaped object can produce lift.

8. The flight of a glider is related to its design.

9. Kites vary in design and purpose.

They will also develop an appreciation for those who "pioneered" flying machines and the importance of flight in their own lives.

Objectives

1. Learn that many people (throughout time) have been, and still are, intrigued by flight.

2. Discover this fascination with flight, which has led to many important inventions and discoveries.

3. Understand that a "pioneer" is someone who breaks new ground for the good of others.

4. Work within a group to use information to create an illustrated, chronological "photo memory poster" about a pioneer of flight.

Resources

Text sets of biographical novels and picture books about pioneers of flight are essential for both classroom (literature circle) use and information processing. These should include such titles as:

>   *Lost Star* (Amelia Earhart)
>
>   *The Glorious Flight* (Charles Lindbergh)
>
>   *Wings* (myths about Icarus)
>
>   *On the Space Shuttle* (Roberta Bondar)
>
>   *Dangerous Adventures* (Wright Brothers)

Other biographies about flight pioneers may cover such people as Leonardo da Vinci, the Montgolfier Brothers, Alexander Graham Bell, Louis Bleriot, Krista McAuliffe, etc.

In addition to these biographical novels and picture books, articles about the "pioneer" will be required. These may be located in an encyclopedia or in children's magazines. Most recently an effort has been made to include electronic encyclopedia articles; the *Encarta* CD-ROM (Microsoft) has been particularly useful. In addition to the audio and visual clips, which add realism to the lives of the "pioneers," (the actual words of Amelia Earhart are quite dramatic!) the classroom teachers have arranged for groups of students to access the CD-ROM work station to learn even more about the scientific principles (such as thrust and lift) that are found in the airplane article. The interactive nature of this information technology ensures maximum involvement for all students. New resources are also available through exciting and worthwhile World Wide Web sites, such as the NASA site. Many other resources (nonfiction books, videos, study prints) were also used in the classroom throughout the flight theme. These were useful for discussions on experiments and inventions. Recommended titles include *Flying Machine, To Space and Back, Why Kites Fly, A Day with an Airplane Pilot, Wings, A Paper Airplane Book, Winging It,* and *How Things Work.* Community resource people, such as airport personnel, amateur pilots, and model plane enthusiasts, can provide interesting input to the theme as well.

Information Skills

Students will activate the information process to learn about a pioneer of flight. If this theme occurs later in the school year, students will enjoy creating this unique product as well as working in a cooperative group setting.

Planning Stage

1.   Following the group's reading and study about one pioneer of flight, create a web (with questions, key words, or categories) to guide their information processing.

Gathering Information

1.   In addition to their group novel (or picture book) the students must access other sources within the information center and in other parts of the library resource center. These will include articles from magazines and encyclopedias, including CD-ROM. (Search terms and magazine and encyclopedia indexes will be used).

2.   Distinguish between relevant and irrelevant information.

Interact with Information

1.   Read, view, or listen to more than one source of information. (Three are required.)

2.   Write concise point-form notes on the web note-taking sheet (by category). Note: See appendix B for a web note-taking form. Each student keeps his or her own sheet in a theme binder.

3.   Make sketches.

4.   Keep track of sources.

Organizing Information

1.   Use the notes to write a short group biography (first draft), which should be two or three pages in length.

2.   Divide the illustration work among the group (based on the web categories, notes, and sketches). These should be chronological, depicting important events, achievements and discoveries. (Up to six "snapshots" will be required.)

Creating New Information

1.   Revise and edit the biography.

2.   Complete a good copy to "publish" on the completed poster.

3.   Choose frames (from shapes provided by teachers—square, oval, hexagon, etc.) for each "snapshot."

4. Finish coloring each "snapshot" and write a brief caption for each illustration.

5. Complete the poster (on colored bristol board) with captioned "snapshots," the biography, a title, and the names of the students in the group.

Sharing/Presenting

1. Share "photo memory" posters by presenting the flight pioneers to classmates or another audience, such as Book Buddies.

2. If a "mini air show" or other flight theme celebration is planned, the posters will make a colorful addition. They may then be displayed in the library resource center for others to appreciate and enjoy.

Evaluating the Process

1. The teacher and teacher-librarian make observations throughout the process to assess the student's information-processing skills and strategies.

2. The students make a group evaluation (see formats in appendix A) to assess the cooperative learning.

3. Teachers also evaluate the products for knowledge and evidence of positive attitudinal outcomes.

Classroom Teacher's Role

1. During the theme the teacher will help students develop an appreciation for the importance of the "pioneers" of flight. This will be accomplished through literature circle discussion, read-aloud selections, science activities, the use of videos, resource people, etc.

2. Select the novels with the teacher-librarian's assistance (about the flight pioneers) and group the students according to reading ability, interest, and other (e.g., social) needs.

3. Assist the teacher-librarian when the information-processing activity is introduced. Retain samples of students' work from previous years to display for students.

4. Contribute new resources (e.g., magazine articles) or recommended new titles for the library resource center collection for the Pioneers of Flight station or for classroom use.

5. Assist students throughout the process (with the teacher-librarian); meet with groups and initial the checkpoints after their note taking is completed, before the groups begin creating their posters.

6. Observe and write notes about students' work. Confer with the teacher-librarian to evaluate individual and group work.

7. Evaluate the completed products (with the teacher-librarian's assistance). Ensure that the evaluation of their information-processing activity becomes a significant part of each student's work when the theme is assessed and when reporting to parents.

Teacher-Librarian's Role

1. Collect and evaluate resources about flight and pioneers of flight. Provide appropriate resources for classroom use and for the Pioneers of Flight information center in the library resource center.

2. Provide an overview (review) of the information process for the students. Describe each stage in terms of the skills and strategies required to process information about pioneers of flight.

3. With the classroom teacher, describe or show the type of products students will create in their groups. It is useful to retain some samples each year for this purpose. Students are then more eager to make their own original products!

4. Assist the classroom teacher throughout the process, by meeting with students and providing instruction for the class or groups as required.

5. Manage the resources in the information station. Ensure that they are readily available for the students' use when needed.

6. Assist the students with processing information from other sources (i.e., searching for, selecting, and interacting with articles from magazines and encyclopedias, including CD-ROM).

7. Assist the teacher by providing observations for the evaluation of the process and the products. Meet with parents during interview times to discuss their children's progress (with regard to information literacy).

8. Display completed "photo memory posters" in the library resource center during or following presentations.

Students' Role

1. Read (in literature circle) and discuss a novel or picture book about a pioneer of flight.

2. Use this reading experience to help design a web about the "pioneer," which will guide the group's information processing.

3. Read, reread, view, and listen to information (including the novel and other sources) about the "pioneer." Write concise notes on the web note-taking sheet and record all sources used.

4. Make sketches of important events, accomplishments, and discoveries, which will assist the group in creating a "photo memory poster."

5. Collaborate within the group by using the collected information and ideas to create a unique and original product.

6. Participate in a group presentation about the "pioneer." Prepare to demonstrate new learning by describing the life and accomplishments of the individual and the efforts of the student group.

Schedule and Activities

This resource-based unit usually begins at the midpoint of the classroom teacher's theme on flight and lasts about two cycles (twelve school days).

Cycle One

Day One
Location: Library resource center

The class visited the library resource center and were asked to sit in their literature circle groups (five or six students per group). The classroom teacher reviewed with each group the "pioneers" of flight they had studied in their novels and picture books. The students were asked why these individuals were considered "pioneers," and responses were discussed as the concept was clarified. The teacher-librarian drew the students' attention to the information station, noting that their literature circle texts and several other resources had been included.

The teachers then explained that each group would be creating a "photo memory poster" about their particular flight pioneer. Several examples of students' work from previous years were displayed, with teachers noting the quality of the products (writing, illustration, neatness, accuracy of information). The resources were then distributed to each group (e.g., all materials pertaining to Amelia Earhart were given to students who had read about her in literature circles). The teacher-librarian noted that, in addition to these articles and videos, study prints, etc., there was much more information available. Students responded with suggestions about using magazine and encyclopedia indexes to locate more articles, as well as accessing the CD-ROM work station. The remainder of the class session was used to read and view these resources. Some students, with supervision, began to search the indexes. Before they left the library resource center, the teacher-librarian asked each group to report their insights about accessing (physically and intellectually) these resources. Students freely gave their comments about using tables of contents, indexes, glossaries, captions, illustrations, etc., and reminded their peers to skim and scan for important facts.

Day Two
Location: Library resource center

The teacher-librarian reviewed the information process, noting the skills and strategies that would be required to complete the activity. The web note-taking format was introduced, and students were asked to consider the categories (or questions or key words) their group would use to collect and organize information.

The students collaborated to design their own webs, with the assistance of the teacher and teacher-librarian. Categories usually included:

personal life/events/qualities,

flight achievements,

recognition and awards, and

other interesting facts.

Students were reminded that *each* person had to complete his or her own note taking (on the single web note-taking sheet) and that three sources were required, including the literature circle novel.

Day Three

The students began their interaction stage. Half the class visited the library (four or five groups), while half remained in the classroom. Those in the library resource center used non-literature circle resources, assisted by the teacher-librarian, while those in the classroom used their texts (novels, picture books), with their teacher's assistance. Both teachers checked the students' note taking to ensure they were recording concise, point-form, relevant information in correct categories.

Day Four

Day three's approach was repeated, reversing the locations for the groups.

Days Five and Six

Students accessed the library resource center in groups throughout the day (using their library resource center passes) and continued to interact with information sources and to write notes and record their sources. By the conclusion of Day Six, most students had their note taking completed, and, after brief conferences in both the classroom and the library resource center, the checkpoint (on the web note-taking sheet) was signed (initialed by the teacher or the teacher-librarian). Note: The resource teacher also provided assistance for students who required support in completing this stage.

Cycle Two

Day One

The class returned to the library resource center and, with the teacher-librarian's direction, focused on the organizing stage of the information process. They were asked to meet within their groups to assess the information they had gathered. Each group was asked to choose one student who would record the first draft of the short (two-page) biography about their pioneer of flight. Other students were expected to contribute facts and ideas as the draft developed (according to the categories in their web). Chronological order was suggested to simplify the process. The classroom teacher reminded the students about earlier biographical writing (an author study) they had completed and recommended using the writing process stages to create an excellent biography for this project. Both the teacher and teacher-librarian met with students and assisted with this stage. It is also possible for the teacher to develop mini-lessons about problematic skills, (such as writing effective introductions and conclusions) as needed.

Day Two

As each group completed their first draft, met with a teacher, and revisions were made, the teacher-librarian met with groups who were ready to begin the "snapshots" (illustration) portion of the activity. Note: Each group chose one student to complete the final editing and completion of the "good copy" of the mini-biography. These were completed in their classrooms at the computer (word-processing) station with assistance provided by the classroom teacher or resource teacher.

Each group delegated one "snapshot" to each student within the group. The typing assignment was an additional responsibility for one student. The teacher-librarian assessed students' sketches and discussed their plans before providing the illustration "frames" (assorted shapes and sizes), which were to be displayed on the bristol board poster.

Days Three, Four, and Five

Student groups worked in their classroom as well as in the library resource center (at times prearranged by the teachers) to complete their illustrations and captions as well as the typed biography. The teachers provided guidance, encouraging their students to reach high standards for content, creativity, and neatness. Both teachers made observations and wrote notes about students' progress.

Day Six

The class met in the library resource center, and most posters were completed, ready for the presentation. The classroom teacher told the students they would be expected to collaborate on their presentations of their "pioneers of flight" for their classmates.

Note: When a "mini air show" is held, the presentations are scheduled for that event. Parents may be invited to this theme celebration.

The teacher-librarian told the students their posters would later be displayed in the library resource center for the rest of the school to enjoy.

A small group evaluation activity was used (see formal suggestions in appendix A). Students were encouraged to assess their own work as well as the contributions of other group members.

Results

This resource-based learning unit took place during the final weeks of the school year. The excitement surrounding the science activities and the principles underlying flight, combined with the students' interest in their "pioneers of flight" resulted in an upbeat theme that was a positive learning experience for everyone. The airport visit, the "mini air show" with students own air machines, and a wonderful kite-making and flying activity were memorable occasions. The students were equally proud of their "photo memory posters"; several groups were pleased to leave their posters for use in later years.

The classroom teacher noted that this particular information-processing activity provided the cooperative learning focus and ample evidence of successfully accomplished learning outcomes that were appreciated by all the educational partners, including parents.

Additional Notes

An alternative approach to this information-processing activity is possible if the students do not have access to the text sets about the pioneers of flight in their language arts program. This biographical information may be made available in the information center, and students may choose one pioneer for their group's project. The literature circle reading and discussion does prepare students to attempt a very thorough study of the flight pioneers.

This theme also provides excellent opportunities to integrate technology. In addition to the word-processing and electronic-encyclopedia (CD-ROM) strategies described here, teachers may collaborate to design a computer database or spreadsheet activity (using ClarisWorks or other programs). The database provides an efficient mechanism for organizing and comparing the attributes of flying machines whereas the spreadsheet allows students to quickly record and calculate numerical data. If, for example, paper airplanes of various designs (or kites or flight machines) are tested, (during activities such as the "mini air show") it is possible to enter their distances and qualities of their flight (such as loops, wobbles, etc.) and determine the most successful designs.

Content-Area Unit:
Social Studies • HELLO CITIES

Background

The study of Canada is a major part of our social studies programs and one that is often stressed in fourth grade. This RBU is one of many developed for primary and intermediate students, and it takes as its focus the Hello Canada series of books published by GLC in 1986. Each book follows a similar format describing a city, such as *Hello Ottawa*, *Hello Toronto*, and *Hello Charlottetown*. A new series, Hello Canada, published by Lerner in 1996 could also be used for this unit of study. Series like these are wonderful resources because they are intellectually accessible for most fourth-grade students, reasonably priced, and useful for teaching how to use a table of contents, an index, and other information-retrieval devices found in good nonfiction materials. They also lend themselves to setting up learning centers and designing resource-based activities.

Goals

The major goal was to provide students with an opportunity to work independently and within cooperative groups to complete resource-based activities on a Canadian city.

Objectives

This RBU was part of a larger social studies theme on Canadian Cities that included a classroom study of our capitol city, Ottawa, classroom activities on Canada's provinces and territories, and the creation of collaborative group displays for the hallway and the learning center in the school library. For this part of the theme, which directly involved the teacher-librarian, the objectives were to have students:

1.   use the table of contents, index, and glossary to access relevant information about the city of choice;

2.   reinforce their concepts of location, population, climate, recreation, industry, places of interest, and entertainment in relation to the city;

3.   record relevant information in point-form notes;

4.   process information about a city in Canada and create an original postcard that would be "posted" to someone on Prince Edward Island; and

5.   use the recorded notes to write an informative message on their postcard and to create the postcard illustration.

Resources

The series Hello Canada (GLC Publishing, 1986) was included in a "Canadian Cities" learning center in the school library resource center. The center also included pictures of Canadian cities, a large map of Canada, a large Canadian flag, posters of major Canadian symbols, and other print and nonprint information about Canada. The commercial software program *World Geography: Canada* was a useful database to make a technology connection. The CD-ROM encyclopedia, *Canadian Encyclopedia Plus* (1997) provided students with an electronic information source.

Booklets that outlined the three activities for students to complete were kept in the learning center, along with blank 5"-x-8" file cards (lined on one side) to be used as their postcards. A copy of the booklet students used to complete their work is included in appendix E. Paper, glue, scissors, markers, etc., were included for illustrating the front of their postcard and for making their individual postage stamps. A mail box was also provided for mailing the completed postcards.

Information Skills

The following information skills were included in this resource-based unit:

1. Use a book's index and glossary.

2. Use a book's table of contents to locate information.

3. Develop techniques to organize and record information.

4. Find specific information by using specialized library materials, including several of the fields and data in a computer program.

Classroom Teacher's Role

As stated above, classroom teachers were working with the students on several other related social studies lessons. For this part of the unit, they had the following responsibilities:

1. to review the concepts of location, climate, industry, population, recreation, and points of interest related to Canadian cities;

2. to check and initial students' notes before they begin writing;

3. to incorporate the teacher-librarian's observations on the completed postcards into the overall evaluation of the unit.

Teacher-Librarian's Role

The teacher-librarian had the following responsibilities:

1. to prepare the Canadian Cities learning center and introduce it to the whole class;

2. to describe for students how they could activate the learning process to complete their postcard from a Canadian city;

3. to review the use of a table of contents, an index, and a glossary;

4. to assist the classroom teacher in checking the notes taken by the student and in helping students with their revising and editing once they were at the writing stage;

5. to track students' use of the learning center and record notes about the completed postcards. These notes will be shared with the classroom teacher as the evaluation of the whole unit is completed.

Students' Role

This whole social studies theme was a busy one for students. The resource-based component of it was lots of fun and filled with opportunities to work independently. Students were expected to do the following:

1. to collect information on a Canadian city and present that information in the form of a postcard written by them from the city of their study back to one of their friends or relatives;

2. to independently complete three activities included in the learning center booklet;

3. to meet with their classroom teacher or the teacher-librarian about their note taking and any revising or editing.

Schedule and Activities

Day One

The whole class visited the school library resource center, and the teacher-librarian introduced the learning center and described how it would operate. Students were introduced to the books they could choose from and shown the three activities they would be expected to complete.

The classroom teacher discussed the concept of sending postcards and showed some real ones. Students brainstormed to list the vital parts of a postcard and recorded what they were to include.

Day Two

Students used their library passes to visit the learning center independently during the school day. They browsed through the learning center, read several of the books, and decided which city they wished to study. A sign-up sheet was provided where they indicated their choice.

Day Three

The classroom teacher reviewed the concepts that students had to know, such as location of the city, population, climate, etc. Time was provided for the students to read in their "Hello Cities" book. Then the teacher-librarian reviewed the use of the major book parts, such as the index, the glossary, etc.

Days Four and Five

Students read and recorded notes in their booklets on the note-taking chart that was provided. The classroom teacher and teacher-librarian worked to have each student's note taking checked and signed before the students move on.

Days Six through Ten

After the note taking had been checked, students wrote messages and made the illustration for their postcards. When this was completed, they addressed the card and made a stamp before "posting" it in the mailbox. This was done during independent visits.

Results

The students really liked the nature of this activity, and they created some very clever postcards. They loved making their own stamps and some even reused the idea in later projects. Coming to the school library resource center in such independent ways and so frequently was also reported as an enjoyable part of this RBU.

Thematic Unit 1: CHILDREN OF THE WORLD

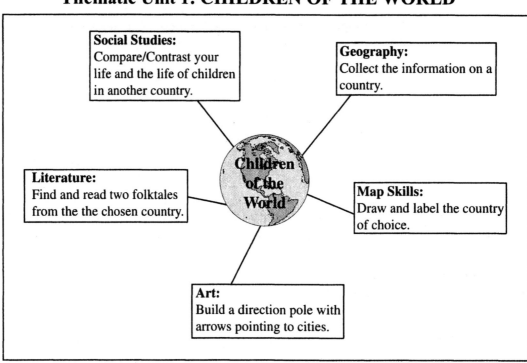

Background

Integrated resource-based units often begin with an isolated subject-area activity and grow into a larger set of interrelated and interconnected activities arising from several concepts teachers want to develop. The web above shows that this basic social studies unit evolved into a more integrated theme centering on the social, cultural, artistic, literary, and geography concepts related to a study of children from various countries of the world. The books from the Gareth Stevens Children of the World series formed the focal point of the theme, with a wide variety of secondary resources incorporated for independent study, such as a database activity using dBase IV, the *MacGlobe* program, and information pulled from the Internet and SchoolNet.

Goals

The major focus of this theme was to develop students' ability to compare and contrast their daily life with the lives of children from other parts of the world. As well, the goal was to have students recognize some of the social, political, and cultural factors that go together to make us who we are.

Objectives

Arising from these general goals, the following specific objectives were outlined:

1. to complete a compare and contrast chart comparing the daily life of children from another country with your own;

2. to develop an understanding of concepts related to daily life, such as home life, school life, hobbies, recreation, and household responsibilities;

3. to find information on one country under the headings of population, government, ethnic groups, religions, education, recreation, natural resources, industries, arts and culture, etc.;

4. to draw and label a map of the same country, including major bodies of water, bordering countries, and major cities;

5. to locate and read two folktales originating in the country studied;

6. to build a direction pole with several arrows pointing the way to travel to get to several places, including the country studied.

Resources

The major resource used was the Children of the World series (Gareth Stevens), which consists of over thirty titles, each one focused on one country. The books are written in a unique style, with the first half concerned with the daily life of a boy or girl of fifth-grade age living in this country. Good photographs and informative text help students enjoy reading about someone their own age. The second part of the books switches tone and gives factual information on the country. Charts, maps, and tables are included as other forms of presenting information. A good table of contents, an extensive index, and a well-organized text with headings and subheadings make these books very useful for supporting students as they read for information.

To support the central role of these Children of the World books, a variety of other books on various countries were provided along with the *MacGlobe* computer program, which allows children to access a wide variety of information on all the countries in the world. This extensive database lets students find their country on a world map, listen to the national anthem of the country, collect facts on the country, and print out a map of the country. Students also used many picture books and fairytale and folktale anthologies to find stories from their chosen country.

Information Skills

Once again during the planning process, the teacher-librarian and the classroom teacher consulted their *Information Skills Continuum* (Province of Prince Edward Island Dept. of Education, 1990) to identify appropriate skills to be taught during this theme. They included:

1. interpreting maps, graphs, and charts;

2. distinguishing between relevant and irrelevant information;

3. making concise notes from various types of resources;

4. distinguishing between fact and opinion; and

5. making a detailed map.

Classroom Teacher's Role

The classroom teacher used the social studies program for fifth grade throughout the year and partnered with the teacher-librarian to provide an independent resource-based unit bringing together their social studies program and language arts. With the whole class or when the class was split in two, the classroom teacher was expected to do the following:

1. to teach several lessons to introduce the theme and reinforce students' understanding of concepts related to information on a country, such as population, geography, capital city, industries, natural resources, manufacturing, recreation, arts and culture, etc.;

2. to develop the concept that all countries have stories and that we can learn about other peoples by reading and sharing their stories;

3. to reinforce their understanding of geographic directions and help students build a large class map of the world with the countries studied highlighted;

4. to read stories from different countries and have students find two stories from their country for their independent literature study;

5. to provide literature-based reading and writing activities focused on the stories of many countries;

6. to respond to students response entries and track their use of the major concepts used to describe a country.

Teacher-Librarian's Role

This theme was developed for fifth-grade students and completed in the spring of the school year. Students were divided into two heterogeneous groups. One worked with the classroom teacher for activities on art and folktales while the other group worked with the teacher-librarian for the activities with the Children of the World books and the *MacGlobe* computer program. Our teaching overlapped in the preparation of students for the social studies and geography activities by the classroom teacher and the information skills taught by the teacher-librarian to enable students complete the art project and their literary study. It was the teacher-librarian's responsibility to do the following:

1. to introduce the Children of the World series and to reinforce the use of tables of contents, indexes, graphs, charts, and other tools for accessing information;

2. to facilitate students' completion of a compare and contrast chart on their daily life and the daily life of a student in their book of choice;

3. to introduce the *MacGlobe* computer program and give students the independent time to find the information on their country and to print out a map;

4. to facilitate the information-processing activity in which students collected factual information from their Children of the World book and completed a fact chart;

5. to assist students as they drew and labeled a map of their country and made a flag;

6. to track student learning with a checklist of skills and checkpoints at major points along the way.

Students' Role

Students were very active and independent in this theme. They came to the library resource center as a group and worked independently on all their activities. They were excited about making the large class map and moved it out into the hallway for display. They added the names of the stories they had read and used string to point to the country the story was from. They were expected to do the following:

1. to read a book of their choice from the Children of the World series;

2. to complete a compare and contrast chart;

3. to complete an information chart with facts on their country;

4. to find their country on the computer program and add any information they found to their chart as well as printing out a map of the country;

5. to draw and label a map and make a flag for their country;

6. to read and respond to two stories from their country;

7. to help build the large wall map and the class direction pole with an arrow giving the number of kilometers to their country and pointed in the right direction.

Schedule and Activities

For three weeks before the theme began, the classroom teacher worked with the social studies program to build the background knowledge that students would need for the more independent work of the theme. Groups were formed and one half of the class went to the library resource center for the work on the computer program or the work on the two charts. The other half stayed in their classroom to work on the literary and art components of the theme. Groups worked in this way alternating for forty-five-minute periods each day for two school weeks. Some students also came extra times through the day on their own to complete work. At the end of the intensive two-week study, the two teachers evaluated progress and made times for the wrap-up and sharing session.

Results

Themes like this one are fairly common in many schools. Students enjoy studies of other countries, especially if they are enhanced with independent work and related to their own daily lives. Educators are emphasizing multicultural studies and a more global perspective in social studies, and this resource-based theme attempted to broaden these concepts by adding the literary and art component. Students enjoyed the Children of the World books very much and delighted in using the *MacGlobe* computer program.

As the theme ended everyone delighted in the large map built in the hallway, and the idea of the direction signs really excited others in the school. Students learned a lot and returned again and again to the library looking for other books on countries around the world.

Thematic Unit 2: PEACE AND FREEDOM

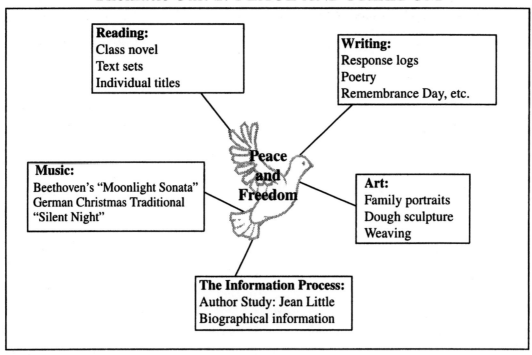

Reading:
Class novel
Text sets
Individual titles

Writing:
Response logs
Poetry
Remembrance Day, etc.

Peace and Freedom

Music:
Beethoven's "Moonlight Sonata"
German Christmas Traditional "Silent Night"

Art:
Family portraits
Dough sculpture
Weaving

The Information Process:
Author Study: Jean Little
Biographical information

Background

During the early part of the school year, many teachers like to develop themes related to peace. It leads nicely into Remembrance Day or Veterans' Day events in early November, and there is a wealth of great children's literature to really give the topic meaning for students. One of the more popular novels that fits this theme well, particularly centered on peace and freedom, is Jean Little's powerful novel *From Anna*. The resource-based unit described here developed out of a larger theme that used this novel as a cornerstone. Other materials were gathered to develop students' understanding of the genre of historical fiction. Students also activated the information process to complete an author study on Jean Little, as well as combining a study of the history, art, and music of Germany. Major concepts developed included immigration, historical fiction, disability, and freedom.

Goals

The major goals for this theme centered on the concept of freedom and the many contexts in which it can be used. Freedom from oppression, freedom of religion and of speech, freedom of movement, and freedom to be yourself were discussed within the framework of World War II and related to our present-day life in this country.

Objectives

Specific objectives grew out of these general goals and included the following:

1. Students will develop an understanding of the importance of freedom in their own lives.

2. Students will develop an appreciation for the writing of Canadian author Jean Little.

3.   Students will activate the information process and complete an author study of Jean Little.

4.   Students will compare and contrast the novel *From Anna* with other novels from the World War II period and develop their understanding of historical fiction.

5.   Students will develop their knowledge of the art and music of Germany.

Resources

To complete the literature components of the theme students were involved in a novel study of *From Anna* by Jean Little. Then they used one of the following titles as the text sets for a literature circle:

Number the Stars by Lois Lowry;

Hockeybat Harris by Geoffrey Bilson;

Sadako and the Thousand Paper Cranes by Eleoner Coerr;

The Devil's Arithmetic by Jane Yolen;

The Upstairs Room by Johanna Reiss;

Different Dragons by Jean Little;

Amish Adventure by Barbara Smucker;

I Dream of Peace by UNICEF;

The Big Book of Peace.

The *Sky Is Falling* by Kit Pearson was used as a read-aloud during the theme. In addition, children read many titles of nonfiction related to World War II and that general time period in history. Teachers also found it useful to read aloud from Jean Little's biography, *Her Special Vision* by Barbara Greenwood.

Other resources included Beethoven's "Moonlight Sonata," the filmstrip and tape telling the *Story of Silent Night*, a *Meet the Author* videotape kit on Jean Little, collective biographies of children's authors, other biographical sources, and all of Jean Little's novels. *Jean: The Story of a Girl* by Gaitskill was used as a picture book read aloud to launch the author study.

Human resources included people from the community who provided information on several German customs, especially Christmas decorations and baking, and who demonstrated weaving and dough sculpture. Community people also spoke to the children about blindness, autism, and physical handicaps.

Information Skills

The following information skills were identified from the school's *Information Skills Continuum.*

1.   Identify different forms of literature, e.g., historical fiction.

2.   Make concise notes from various types of resources.

3.   Recognize the role fiction plays as a source of information.

4.   Write a content-related report that includes a title page and bibliography.

Classroom Teacher's Role

This theme was a focus of several weeks work in the classroom. The teacher used literature circles as a strategy for discussion of the novels read and had students use several writing strategies to develop their response. The major components of the classroom teacher's role included the following:

1. to organize students into literature circles for discussing and sharing their ideas on the major concepts developed in the theme;

2. to develop activities that encourage student response to the reading of *From Anna* and the other text sets;

3. to cooperatively teach students how to complete an author study;

4. to meet with students at several points throughout the information process and provide feedback on their progress;

5. to share in the evaluation of students' completed biographies on the author.

Teacher-Librarian's Role

A large part of the theme was developed in the classroom during the literature studies. When students were ready to complete the author study, the teacher-librarian became directly involved. In addition, the teacher-librarian was involved during the visits of community resource people, the completion of art and music activities, and the closing events of the theme. The following activities were specific to the teacher-librarian:

1. to introduce and explain the information station located in the school library for all materials related to Jean Little;

2. to teach note-taking strategies to be used during the author study;

3. to introduce the information process and show students how they will use the "Students Guide to Completing an Author Study" (fig. 2.14, pages 50-57);

4. to assist the classroom teacher in monitoring students' progress through the author study;

5. to meet with students as they prepare written reports on the author;

6. to assist students as they complete art and music activities arising from guest speakers' presentations on the customs of Germany.

Students' Role

Students were very interested in the time period of the novel *From Anna* and quite fascinated with its author Jean Little. They read many of her other books and used the literature circles as a forum for sharing their ideas on the major themes of the unit. These were their specific responsibilities:

1. to read several titles in the historical fiction genre and from the nonfiction materials provided for this topic;

2. to complete the "Student's Guide to Completing an Author Study" (fig. 2.14) and write a biography of Jean Little;

3. to discuss in their literature circles ideas from the novels and personal responses to their reading;

4. to keep a response log on their reading;

5. to take part in several art and music activities related to the customs of Germany.

Schedule and Activities

For three weeks the students worked in their classrooms reading, writing, and talking about the novel *From Anna*. Then they chose a text set group and began an independent study of that novel. All the time, they kept a response log and read other books independently. At the beginning of the fourth week, they began their author study of Jean Little and became directly involved with the teacher-librarian.

The teacher-librarian introduced the information station in the school library and reviewed what was involved in the information process and how they were going to track their way through the process using the "Student's Guide to Completing an Author Study" (fig. 2.14). The guide was designed to help them understand all parts of the process and to keep them aware of what they had completed and what was left to be done.

In a subsequent session students reviewed the note-taking procedure and viewed the video on Jean Little. They returned several times to collect more information from materials in the information station. The teacher-librarian and the classroom teacher met with students at three checkpoints along the way. They checked their categorization of notes, the outlines the students made from their notes, and the students' first drafts.

Once the author study was completed, arrangements were made for the community resource people to visit and share their information on the many customs of Germany. Students took part in several art activities, including painting a family portrait using watercolors, making a German dough and using it for sculpture, and weaving. During music classes the works of Beethoven were shared as well as information on how the famous Christmas song "Silent Night" was written.

Students created hallway displays on the life and works of Jean Little and displayed their written biographies. Many of the responses they created were shared during Remembrance Day activities.

Results

Students take themes like this very seriously. They have strong feelings about war, peace, and freedom, and they respond well to discussions about life during the difficult times of World War II. It is also an easy step for them to take these concepts and relate them to issues of personal freedom and acceptance of others. There are many well-written books on this theme and lots of poetry to help teachers bring these issues into the context of today's world.

During the writing of the rough drafts, the classroom teacher and the teacher-librarian noticed students were having trouble writing good openings for their biographies. Several writing lessons were held to teach students some of the strategies that might help their opening and closing paragraphs. Here are two examples of an opening and then one of a closing paragraph written by children during this theme.

Jean Little is liked by thousands of people. She writes books that encourage people to accept others as they are.

Crystal, age 10

Jean Little is one of the world's greatest authors for children and adults. She writes exciting stories about friendship and children with problems.

Jill, age 11

From the time she wrote her first book in an orange scribbler in grade five, to her latest book, *Jess Was the Brave One*, Jean Little's books have been loved not only by Canadians, but by people all over the world. I hope she writes many more books.

Megan, age 11

Summary

In chapter 3 we have attempted to provide classroom teachers with several examples of how they may activate their partnership with the teacher-librarian and develop exciting and purposeful activities that will allow students to develop all aspects of their literacy. The examples fall into one of three categories—activities centered on resources, those promoting literacy, and those activating the information process through resource-based units. These examples barely scratch the surface of what can be done, and they are certainly not meant to represent an exhaustive list. Hopefully they give all teachers confidence that they too can engage in resource-based learning and that by working together, we can greatly enhance and enrich the literacy experiences of our students.

CHAPTER FOUR

Some Final Thoughts on the Partnership

We are in the process of many changes in education. Every day the cry goes out for our schools to become more effective and more responsive to the needs of society. The demands on teachers seem to grow with each new school year and students are expected to develop more and more skills to be able to take their place in the adult world as productive, knowledgeable, capable, and literate citizens.

Developing hand-in-hand with these growing demands and pressures have been new understandings of how learning happens and what strategies teachers can apply to affect student learning. We know that learning is an active process and that it develops in social situations where students have opportunities to interact around shared experiences. Students must feel that they are part of the learning process and that they have some control of the learning situation. They ought to work cooperatively with peers and teachers to apply critical-thinking skills and solve problems. They need to develop their skills at using information critically and for informed purposes. Taken together, these principles inform teachers that the classroom cannot be confined to the space of four walls. Students must reach out into the world for the knowledge that allows them to practice the literacy skills essential for life in an information-rich future. As teachers, we must work together to help students seek that knowledge and guide them as they develop and practice the skills and strategies they will need to evaluate the information and use it in their daily lives.

This book has attempted to show classroom teachers and teacher-librarians how they can work together with students and the varied resources of the school library resource center to build a literacy program rich in active, student-centered, resource-based learning. It is a demonstration of what can happen when the educational partners activate a collaborative relationship and work together to realize common goals and shared objectives. With the commitment to such a relationship, the rewards are multiplied and a strong literacy program is assured.

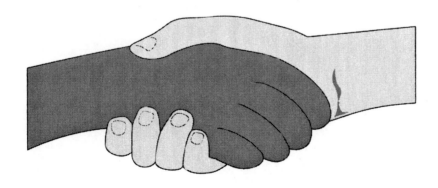

Appendix A

Evaluation and Assessment Forms

Group Evaluations: Student Samples and
Blank Form

Project Assessment: Student Sample and
Blank Form

Peer Evaluation of Group Presentations:
Blank Form

GROUP EVALUATION

Group Members: Wade

Christopher, Jayne

Name: Christopher

Date: January 27/92

Project: _____

1. Did your group experience any difficulties with the assignment? If so, what were they?
At first we had trouble making our model. Before that Wade was away so Jayne and I had to hope he would like our ideas. Sometimes but not very often Jayne got a little bossy. But the hardest part was making the beds for the model.

2. How did *YOU* help solve these problems? I tried to improve the model over the holidays with the help of my mother and father.

3. Was the work distributed fairly? Yes, but Jayne and I had a little harder work when Wade was away.

4. If not, how could this problem be overcome? _____

5. What did *YOU* do to help complete the assignment? I typed the question sheet and the report.

6. What did you learn from the assignment? I found out it was alot of fun to be the only mixed boy and girl group

7. Assign a mark out of 5 for each member of your group, bearing in mind their efforts toward completing this assignment. In the space provided, justify the mark you have given with reasons for that mark.

NAME: __Jayne_____ Mark   5/5
She worked hard alot of the time and she didn't mind writing the rough copie.
_____
_____
_____

NAME: ___Wade_____ Mark   5/5
He worked fairly hard through the time that he was there. but when the gluegun was
_here he started to fool around with it._____
_____
_____

NAME: _Christopher_____ Mark   5/5
I worked hard as I could to make the project look nice for displaying in the hall but I
_fooled around a little too._____
Really we all fooled around sometimes because life isn't work. People need to play too!
_____

NAME:_____ Mark   /5
_____
_____
_____
_____

NAME:_____ Mark   /5
_____
_____
_____
_____

GROUP EVALUATION

Group Members: _wade_ **Name:** _wade_

christopher jayne **Date:** _january 27/92_

_____ **Project:** _____

1. Did your group experience any difficulties with the assignment? If so, what were they?
yes we had trouble building our hospice

2. How did *YOU* help solve these problems? _i helped make different ways to build_
the hospice

3. Was the work distributed fairly? _yes it was_

4. If not, how could this problem be overcome? _____

5. What did *YOU* do to help complete the assignment? _i answered all of my_
questions and helped complete the hospice

6. What did you learn from the assignment? _i learned how to work better in_
groups and about the middle ages

7. Assign a mark out of 5 for each member of your group, bearing in mind their efforts toward completing this assignment. In the space provided, justify the mark you have given with reasons for that mark.

NAME: _wade_____ Mark   5/5

i got 4/5 because i helped with the hospice and the good copy

NAME: ___christopher_____ Mark   5/5

he got 5/5 because he did alot at home

NAME: _jayne_____ Mark   5/5

she got 5/5 because she wrote up the rough copy and helped make the hospice

NAME:_____ Mark   /5

NAME:_____ Mark   /5

GROUP EVALUATION

Group Members: _____ **Name:** _Jayne_ _____

_____ _Wade_   _Jayne_   _Christopher_   **Date:** _____ _January 27/92_ _____

_____ **Project:** _____

1. Did your group experience any difficulties with the assignment? If so, what were they?
Well we had difficulties finding information. Because we did medicine and cures, and trying to make a
model. And when we tried to make beds.

2. How did *YOU* help solve these problems? _Yes I did. I helped look for more information. And_
helped to make the beds.

3. Was the work distributed fairly? _I would say yes the work was fair._

4. If not, how could this problem be overcome? _____

5. What did *YOU* do to help complete the assignment? _We got Mr. McD to get the questionare_
copyed and help set it up.

6. What did you learn from the assignment? _Well what I learned about myself I can become_
somewhat bossy. And I need to try to understand the people with me in a group. And I have to work
with other's better.

7. Assign a mark out of 5 for each member of your group, bearing in mind their efforts toward completing this assignment. In the space provided, justify the mark you have given with reasons for that mark.

NAME: _Christopher_   Mark   5/5

I gave Chris this mark because Chris worked very hard on this project to learn and understand more.

_____

_____

_____

NAME: _Wade_   Mark   4/5

I gave Wade this mark because it seemed he was getting a little impatient.

_____

_____

_____

NAME: _Jayne_   Mark   3/5

Because I felt that I did a little on the project. But I did do about half.

_____

_____

_____

NAME:_____   Mark   /5

_____

_____

_____

_____

NAME:_____   Mark   /5

_____

_____

_____

_____

GROUP EVALUATION

Group Members:_____ **Name:**_____
_____ **Date:**_____
_____ **Project:**_____

1. Did your group experience any difficulties with the assignment? If so, what were they?
_____
_____
_____
_____

2. How did *YOU* help solve these problems? _____
_____
_____
_____

3. Was the work distributed fairly? _____
_____

4. If not, how could this problem be overcome? _____
_____
_____
_____

5. What did *YOU* do to help complete the assignment? _____
_____
_____

6. What did you learn from the assignment? _____
_____
_____
_____

7. Assign a mark out of 5 for each member of your group, bearing in mind their efforts toward completing this assignment. In the space provided, justify the mark you have given with reasons for that mark.

NAME:_____ Mark   /5

_____

_____

_____

_____

NAME:_____ Mark   /5

_____

_____

_____

_____

NAME:_____ Mark   /5

_____

_____

_____

_____

NAME:_____ Mark   /5

_____

_____

_____

_____

NAME:_____ Mark   /5

_____

_____

_____

_____

PROJECT ASSESSMENT

Title: Jean Little, Canines, Computers and Covers   **Grade:** 5

Name: Gregory

V.G. = very good   **S** = satisfactory   **E.D.** = experiencing difficult   **N.I.** = needs improvement

Sections	Rating Code	Student Comments	Rating Code	Teacher(s) / Teacher-Librarian Comments
Cover	V.G.	I think it was quite neat and colorful.	VG	I do like your title! Please write your name and date on the title page.
Introduction	V.G.	My introduction had quite a lot of info.	S	I'm not sure if the "rainbow" on the title page includes your introduction...or is it the first paragraph on page one?
Information Process	S	I don't think my process was that good.	S	I agree (partly). You know I was concerned that you didn't use enough sources, with so many available! You also had to concentrate on reading and writing more notes. The rest of the process went quite well and would have been more satisfying for you if the first stages had received more attention.
Product	V.G.	I think that my final copy was quite good and informitive.	S	Nicely written (including revision and editing) Thank you for a fine biography Greg. Please use a ruler for underlining.
Illustrations	S	I'm not a good drawer so my perfect illustrations aren't great.	S	Your illustrations are very helpful for the reader, they enhance the biography
Conclusions	S	My conclusion is an okay job, the poem.	S	I agree, she is "amazing". Perhaps you could tell the reader why you chose the poem "Oranges" or why you think she's a great author. I think you learned alot about the information process & we learned alot about each other.

Parent's Comments   I found this project quite an undertaking for 10 year olds. It certainly proved to be a learning process for everyone! Gregory worked very hard, and his father and I are very pleased with his effort.

Parent's Signature   Mrs. C.

PROJECT ASSESSMENT

Title: _____   **Grade:** _____

Name: _____

V.G. = very good   **S** = satisfactory   **E.D.** = experiencing difficult   **N.I.** = needs improvement

Sections	_Rating Code_	_Student Comments_	_Rating Code_	_Teacher(s) / Teacher-Librarian Comments_
Cover				
Introduction				
Information _Process_				
Product				
Illustrations				
Conclusions				

Parent's Comments _____

_____

Parent's Signature _____

PEER EVALUATION OF GROUP PRESENTATIONS

Observer's Name: _____

Group Observed: _____

	Evident	Not Evident
* Was organized and prepared for the Presentation	_____	_____
* Was knowledgeable about topic	_____	_____
* Demonstrated an ability to work together as a group	_____	_____
* Presented information in a logical way	_____	_____
* Was creative in their presentation	_____	_____
* Stayed on topic	_____	_____
* Encouraged participation from the audience	_____	_____

Strengths of the Presentation

_____

_____

_____

_____

_____

_____

_____

Suggestions for Improvement

_____

_____

_____

_____

_____

_____

_____

Appendix B

Guides and Organizers

Bibliography Guides

Notes Organizer

Fact Sheet Form

Fact-Finding Guide—Children of the World: Blank Forms

Note-Taking Web: Sample and Blank Form

BIBLIOGRAPHY SHEET

AUTHOR:_____   AUTHOR:_____

TITLE:_____   TITLE:_____

OTHER TITLE:_____   OTHER TITLE:_____

_____   _____

PUBLISHER:_____   PUBLISHER:_____

DATE:_____   DATE:_____

VOLUME:_____   VOLUME:_____

FORMAT:_____   FORMAT:_____

AUTHOR:_____   AUTHOR:_____

TITLE:_____   TITLE:_____

OTHER TITLE:_____   OTHER TITLE:_____

_____   _____

PUBLISHER:_____   PUBLISHER:_____

DATE:_____   DATE:_____

VOLUME:_____   VOLUME:_____

FORMAT:_____   FORMAT:_____

REMINDER: "Other Titles" means title of encyclopedia or magazine.

BIBLIOGRAPHY GUIDE FOR ELEMENTARY STUDENTS

1. FOR A BOOK:
Author, <u>Title,</u> Publisher, Copyright date.
> Example:
> Taylor, Dave, <u>Endangered Desert Animals</u>, Crabtree Publishing Company, 1993.

2. FOR AN ENCYCLOPEDIA:
> "Article," <u>Encyclopedia Name</u>, Volume Number, (last copyright date).
> Example:
> "Wind Energy," <u>The Junior Encyclopedia of Canada</u>, Volume Five, 1990.

3. FOR A MAGAZINE ARTICLE OR PAMPHLET:
> Author (if known), "Article," <u>Magazine Name</u>, Date.
> Example:
> "Ghostly Warwick Castle," <u>National Geographic World</u>, September, 1993.

4. FOR A FILMSTRIP OR VIDEO (OR AUDIOCASSETTE OR STUDY PRINT):
> "Title of filmstrip or video," <u>Title of Series</u> (Filmstrip or Video or Audiocassette or Study Print).
> Example:
> "Endangered Animals," <u>A Look Around</u> (Video).

5. FOR A HUMAN RESOURCE: (PERSON)
> Last Name, First Name, Position or Relationship, Date of Visit or Interview.
> Example:
> Kissick, Barbara, Children's Librarian, Confederation Centre Public Library, November 15, 1995.

6. FOR AN ELECTRONIC RESOURCE:
> (COMPUTER SOFTWARE)
> Name of the Software Company, "Title of Software," (Computer Software)
>
> (CD-ROM)
> Author (if known, last namefirst), "Article," Title of CD-ROM, (last copyright date)
>
> (ONLINE DATABASE)
> Author (if known, last name first), "Article," Title of Publication or Website, (date published or posted), Online Source (e.g. Internet or other network), date you used this material.

From *Partners in Learning*. Copyright © 1998 Ray Doiron and Judy Davies. Libraries Unlimited. (800) 237-6124.

ORGANIZING YOUR NOTES
Topic: _____

Subtopic/Category

Subtopic/Category

_____
_____
_____
_____
_____
_____
_____

_____
_____
_____
_____
_____
_____
_____

Subtopic/Category

Subtopic/Category

_____
_____
_____
_____
_____
_____
_____

_____
_____
_____
_____
_____
_____
_____

Subtopic/Category

Subtopic/Category

_____
_____
_____
_____
_____
_____
_____

_____
_____
_____
_____
_____
_____
_____

**CHECKPOINT #1 After you have organized your notes
have a teacher sign here** _____

FACT SHEET

Name:_____ Topic: _____

FACT FINDING GUIDE • CHILDREN OF THE WORLD

Student's Name:_____ Teacher's Name:_____Date:_____

Country:	**Official Name:**
Capital City:	**Population:**
Currency:	**Ethnic Groups:**
Languages:	**Religions:**
Natural Resources:	**Industries:**
Land:	**Climate:**
Education:	**Recreation:**
Government:	**Flag:** ⟶ (draw and color this country's flag in this box)
Other Interesting Facts:	

From *Partners in Learning*. Copyright © 1998 Ray Doiron and Judy Davies. Libraries Unlimited. (800) 237-6124.

ONE WORLD • MANY CULTURES : A COMPARE AND CONTRAST ACTIVITY

Name:		
Country:		
Town or Community:		
House:		
Family Life:		
School Life:		
Recreation:		
Special Days:		
Other Interesting Facts:		

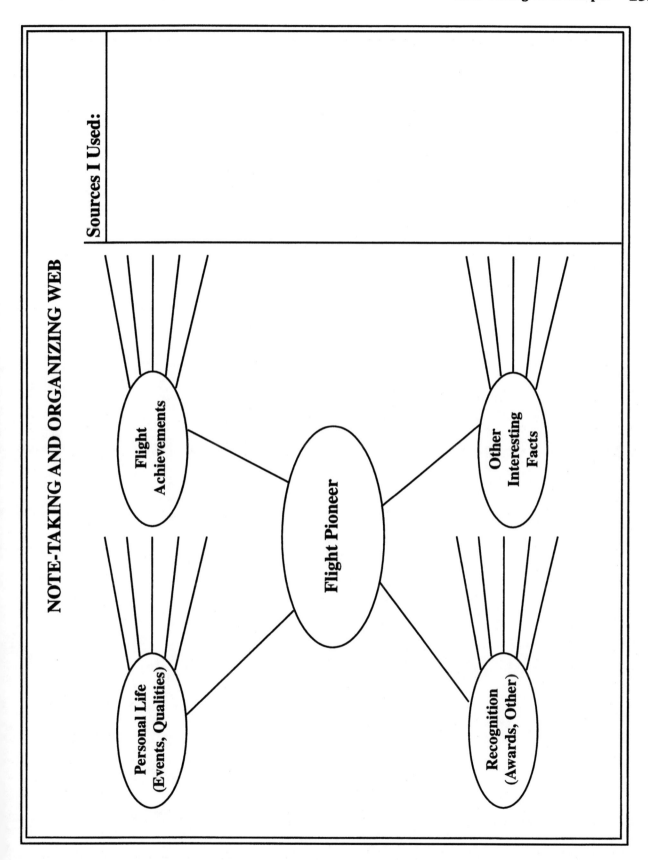

NOTE-TAKING AND ORGANIZING WEB

Sources I Used:

Flight Achievements

Other Interesting Facts

Flight Pioneer

Personal Life (Events, Qualities)

Recognition (Awards, Other)

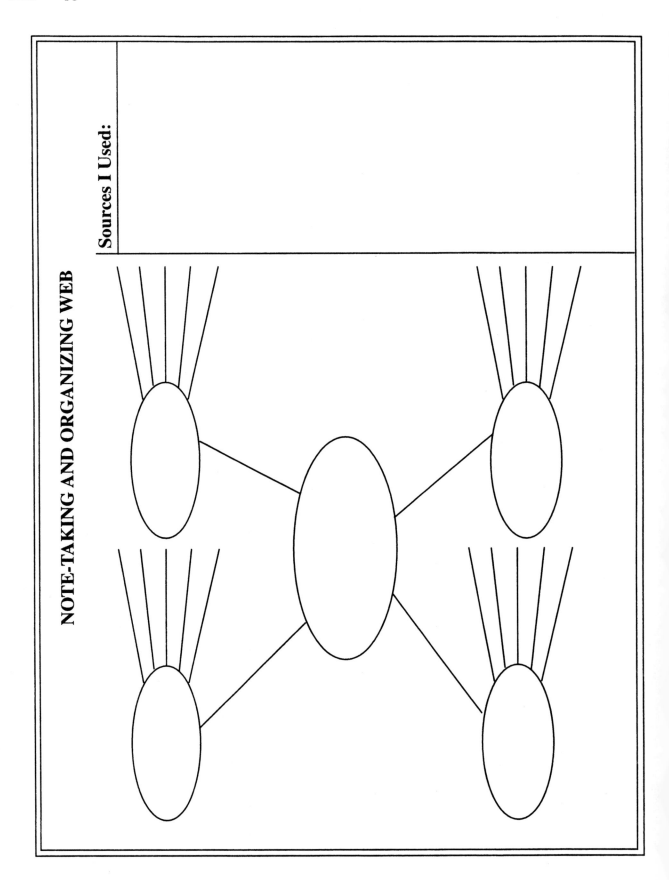

NOTE-TAKING AND ORGANIZING WEB

Sources I Used:

Appendix C

Projects, Presentations, and Student Products

Projects, Presentations, and Student Products

Articles • for a newspaper or magazine
Artifacts • make replicas of artifacts based on research
Advertisements • visual as in a poster; or oral, as in radio; videotaped, as for TV
Big Book Productions
Banners, Bulletins, and Broadcasts
Biographies
Books, Bookcovers, and Bookmarks
Brochures and Information handout • on research topics
Bulletin Boards • students prepare a bulletin board display on their topic
Cartoons
Cassette Tapes • audio and/or visual
Charts
Collages
Debates
Demonstrations
Diaries
Drama Presentations
Editorials
Essays
Experiments
Films, Filmstrips
Games • create your own games
Graphs
Guided Tours, Guidebooks
Interviews
Illustrations
Jingles • for advertisements and promotions
Job Applications
Letters
Lists
Logbooks
Manuals
Maps
Masks
Memoirs
Mobiles, Models
Murals
Overhead Transparencies

Pamphlets
Photographs
Pictures • with captions
Plays
Poetry
Posters • use poster to show research results
Puppet Shows
Puzzles • make a math or jigsaw puzzle
Quiz, Tests • create your own exam to include the information you found
Recitations, Choral Readings
Reports • oral and written
Reporter • to be a reporter and report data discovered
Resumes
Reviews • of books or presentations
Slogans • capture the essence of your research in a catchy slogan
Songs
Speeches
Survey • collect data on a set of questions and report results
Tables • display information collected
Time Lines
Teach • teach your research results to others
Word Searches
Videos • prepare an instructional video of the information

Appendix D

Amazing Animals Booklet

AMAZING ANIMALS

Name:

Teacher:

Date:

ACTIVITY ONE

Title of the Book: _____ Author: _____

Publisher of the Book: _____ Publication Year: _____

ACTIVITY TWO

Title of the Book: _____ Author: _____

Publisher of the Book: _____ Publication Year: _____

ACTIVITY THREE

Title of the Book: _____ Author: _____

Publisher of the Book: _____ Publication Year: _____

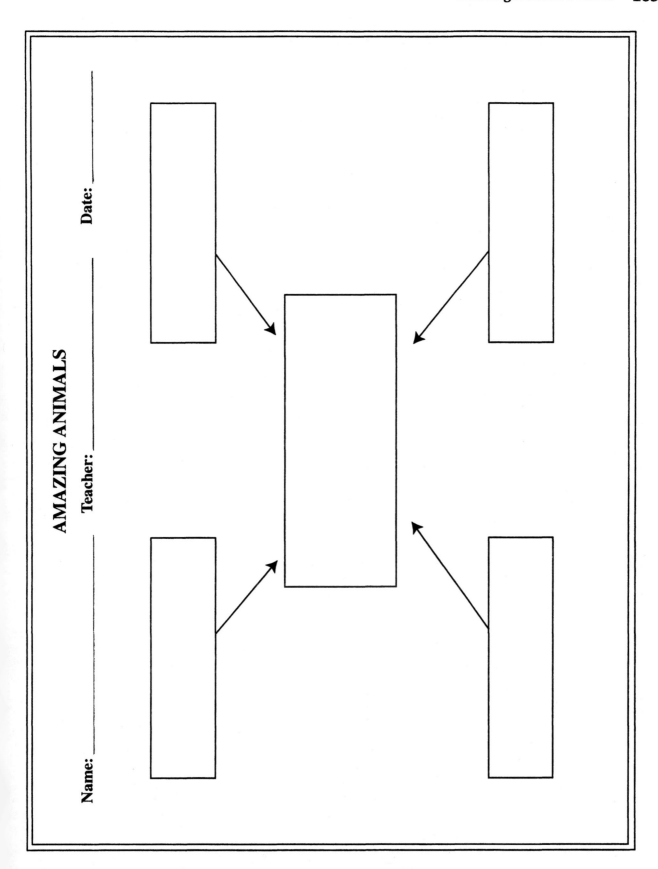

AMAZING ANIMALS

Name: _____

Teacher: _____

Date: _____

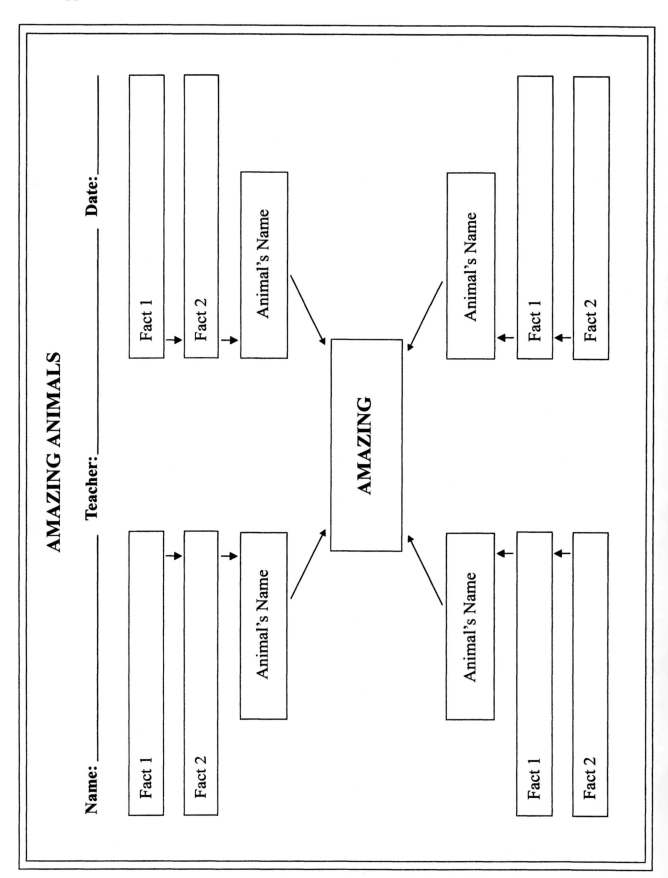

Appendix E

Canada Theme Booklet for Hello Canada Series

L.M. MONTGOMERY GRADE FOUR
CANADA THEME

LIBRARY-RESOURCE CENTRE ACTIVITIES

ACTIVITY 1

MAKING A POSTCARD ABOUT A CANADIAN CITY
(Resource: Hello Canada Series)

a. Choose one book about a city in Canada.

_____

(Title)   (Author)

_____

(Publisher)   (Copyright Date)

b. Read the book. How is the information organized?

Table of Contents   _____

Index   _____

Glossary   _____   (Yes or No)

Illustrations   _____

Maps/Graphs/Charts   _____

c. Write point-form notes (at least one fact about each of the following subtopics):

(location)	(climate)
(place(s) of interest)	(recreation)
(industry)	(your choice)

CHECKPOINT 1:	
	Teacher or Teacher-Librarian's Initials

Pretend you are visiting the city and that you want to send a postcard to a relative or friend back home in Prince Edward Island.

d. Take one card. Use the illustrations in the book to help you decide on the illustration you will draw and color on the front of your postcard.

e. Tell where the card is from. (Greetings From) _____
Write a title under your picture (about the illustration). Print neatly!

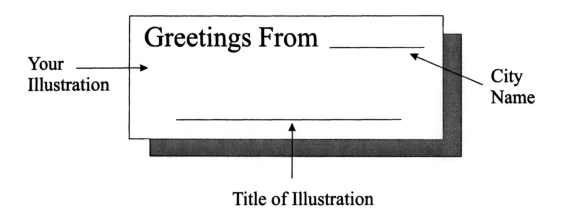

f. Decide on what information you will include in the message on the back of
your postcard. (Use your notes.) Write the rough draft for your message here:

Dear _____   _____

                                              (Date)

_____

_____

_____

_____

_____

_____

_____

_____

_____

_____

_____

_____

_____

g. Write the name and address of the person in P.E.I. who will receive your card:

Name: _____

Address: _____

_____

_____

_____

_____

_____

_____

CHECKPOINT 2:	
	Teacher or Teacher-Librarian's Initials

h. Now write the message on the back of your postcard and add the name and address as well. Place a stamp on the card and "mail it" by placing it in the post box in the Information Centre.

EXAMPLE

(Message)   (Name, Address)

References

Professional References

American Association of School Libraries and Association for Educational Communications and Technology. 1988. *Information Power: Guidelines for School Library Media Programs*. Chicago: American Library Association.

Barton, Bob, and David Booth. 1990. *Stories in the Classroom: Storytelling, Reading Aloud and Roleplaying with Children*. Markham, Ont.: Pembroke.

Canadian School Library Association. 1988. *Guidelines for Effective School Library Programs*. Occasional Paper #1. Rationale, Ottawa, Ont.: Canadian School Library Association.

Hart-Hewins, Linda, and Jan Wells. 1992. *Read It in the Classroom! Organizing an Interactive Language Arts Program Grades 4-9*. Markham, Ont.: Pembroke.

Haycock, Carol-Ann. 1991. "Resource-Based Learning: A Shift in the Roles of Teacher, Learner." *NASSP Bulletin* 75, no. 535 (May): 15-22.

Haycock, Ken, ed. 1990. *The School Library Program in the Curriculum*. Englewood, Colo.: Libraries Unlimited.

Province of Ontario Ministry of Education. 1982. *Partners in Action*. Toronto: Province of Ontario Ministry of Education.

Province of Prince Edward Island Department of Education. 1990. *Information Skills Continuum*. Charlottetown, P.E.I.: Province of Prince Edward Island Department of Education.

Bibliography of Children's Titles

Aliki. *A Medieval Feast*. New York: Thomas Y. Crowell, 1983.

The Big Book of How Things Work. Lincolnwood, Ill.: Publications International, 1991.

Bilson, Geoffrey. *Goodbye Sarah*. Toronto: Kids Can Press, 1981.

———. *Hockeybat Harris*. Toronto: Kids Can Press, 1984.

Bondar, Roberta. *On the Shuttle: Eight Days in Space*. Toronto: Greey de Pencier Books, 1993.

Bulla, Clyde Robert. *The Sword in the Tree*. New York: Crowell/HarperCollins, 1956.

Byars, Betsy. *The Midnight Fox*. New York: Viking, 1968.

———. *The Summer of the Swans*. New York: Viking, 1970.

Coerr, Eleanor. *Sadako and the Thousand Paper Cranes*. New York: Putnam, 1977.

de Angeli, Marguerite. *The Door in the Wall*. New York: Doubleday, 1949.

Dwiggins, Don. *Why Kites Fly*. London: Rejensteiner, 1976.

Gaitskell, Susan. *A Story of Jean*. Toronto: Oxford University Press, 1989.

Gray, Elizabeth Janet. *Adam of the Road*. New York: Viking, 1942.

Greenwood, Barbara. *Her Special Vision: A Biography of Jean Little*. Toronto: Irwin, 1987.

Greer, Gery. *Max and Me and the Time Machine*. New York: Harcourt Brace Jovanovich, 1983.

Haddrell, Allan, and Christine Haddrell. *A Day with an Airplane Pilot*. East Sussex, England: Wayland, 1980.

Hastings, Selina. *Sir Gawain and the Loathly Lady*. New York: Lothrop, Lee and Shepard, 1985.

I Dream of Peace: Images of War by Children of Former Yugoslavia. New York: HarperCollins, 1994.

Ingle, Annie, adapter. *Robin Hood*. A Bullseye Step into Classics. New York: Random House, 1991.

Hodges, Margaret. *Saint George and the Dragon: A Golden Legend*. New York: Little, Brown, 1984.

Lasker, Joe. *Merry Ever After: The Story of Two Medieval Weddings*. New York: Viking, 1976.

Lasky, Kathryn. *The Night Journey*. Markham, Ont.: Penguin Books, 1972.

Lauber, Patricia. *Lost Star*. New York: Scholastic, 1988.

Little, Jean. *Different Dragons*. New York: Viking, 1986.

———. *From Anna*. New York: HarperCollins, 1972.

Lowry, Lois. *Number the Stars*. Boston: Houghton Mifflin, 1989.

Mowat, Farley. *Owls in the Family*. New York: Little, Brown, 1961.

Munsch, Robert N. *Mud Puddle*. Toronto: Annick Press, 1982.

———. *Show and Tell*. Toronto: Annick Press, 1991.

Nathun, Andrew. *Flying Machine*. Eyewitness Books. Toronto: Stoddart, 1990.

Pearson, Kit. *The Sky Is Falling*. Toronto: Viking Kestrel, 1989.

Provenson, Martin, and Alice Provenson. *The Glorious Flight*. New York: Viking, 1983.

Reiss, Johanna. *The Upstairs Room*. New York: Thomas Y. Crowell, 1972.

Ride, Sally, and Susan Okie. *To Space and Back*. New York: Lothrop, Lee and Shepard, 1986.

Smucker, Barbara. *Amish Adventure*. Toronto: Clark Irwin, 1983.

Stevenson, Augusta. *Wilbur and Orville Wright: Young Fliers*. New York: Simon and Schuster Children's Publishing, 1986.

Stone, Lynn. *Owls*. Vero Beach, Fla.: Rourke Enterprises, 1989.

Tejima, Keizaburo. *Owl Lake*. New York: Philomel, 1987.

Winthrop, Elizabeth. *The Castle in the Attic*. New York: Holiday House, 1985.

Yolen, Jane. *The Devil's Arithmetic*. New York: Viking, 1988.

———. *Wings*. New York: Harcourt Brace Jovanovich, 1991.

Series

Canada Rainbow Series. Hello Cities. Individual titles dealing with different Canadian cities. Order book by city name.

- Schemenauer, Elma. *Hello Charlottetown*. Toronto: GLC/Silver Burdett, 1986.

Children of the World Series. Individual titles dealing with a different country. Order book by series name and country name.

- Wright, David K. *Canada*. Milwaukee: Gareth Stevens Books, 1991.

Eyewitness Juniors. Amazing Worlds Series. Individual titles dealing with a different animal or type of animal. Order book by animal name.

- Ling, Mary. *Amazing Fish*. London: Stoddart. 1991.
- Parsons, Alexandra. *Amazing Birds*. London: Stoddart/Knopf, 1990.

Hello Canada Series. Individual books dealing with each province and territory in Canada. Order book by name of province or territory.

- Campbell, Kumari. *Prince Edward Island*. Minneapolis, Minn.: Lerner, 1995.

Audio-Visual and Computer Resources

Canadian Encyclopedia Plus. (CD-ROM). Toronto: McClelland and Stewart, 1997.

Gallico, Paul W. *The Story of Silent Night*. (Sound Filmstrip). Portsmouth, N.H.: Heinemann, 1967.

MacGlobe, Version 1.0. Tempe, Arizona: PC Globe, 1991.

Meet the Author: Jean Little.(Sound Filmstrip). Toronto: Mead Sound Filmstrips, 1987.

Meet the Author: Robert Munsch. (Sound Filmstrip). Toronto: Mead Sound Filmstrips, 1987.

Mind's Eye: Jean Little. (Videotape).Toronto: School Services of Canada, 1994.

Index

Research
skills. *See* Information skills
traditional vs. process-oriented projects, 35–36
Resource-based learning, 7
advantage for students, 17
information process and, 35–38
as learning strategy, 16
model, 7–8
partnership with curriculum, 4
vs. resource-based teaching, 16–17
structured learning stations and, 18
student's guide for author study, 50–57fig.
unit for fourth-grade students (Owls), 19–22
Resource-based programs
curriculum development and, 8
instruction of information skills and, 10
Resource-based study units, 85
content area, 101–17
literary, 86–100
resource center development and, 3–4
thematic, 118–27. *See also specific areas of study units, e.g.,* Goals (in study units); Information skills (in study units)
Resource center, collection location in, 11
Resource center program
administrative support for, 24
collaborative program planning, teaching, and evaluation, 22–26
information skills and, 12
learning strategies for, 16
materials for independent use, 61–64
materials for instructional use, 61, 64–68
reading aloud and, 68–69
Resources
access to, 2, 8, 43
access via interlibrary loan, 11
appropriateness for students, 18
classroom teachers and use of, 6–7
effective use of, 10–11, 16
for instructional use, 61, 64–68
formats of, 10–11
identification of, 26
impact of information technologies, 2
integration with curriculum, 4
meeting demand, 60
organization of, 66
planning for acquisition of, 61–68
planning for selection of, 64
resource-based learning and use of, 16
students demand for, 9

students interaction with, 44
types of collections, 7. *See also specific resource, e.g.,* Video resources
Resources (in study units)
content area units, 102, 107–8, 115
literary units, 87, 95
Results (in study units)
content area units, 104, 113, 117
literary units, 94, 99–100
thematic units, 121, 126–27
Retrieval, instruction in, 3. *See also* Access
Review. *See* Evaluation

Satellites, accessibility and, 2
Schedule and activities (in study units)
content area units, 103–4, 111–13
literary units, 90–94, 97–99, 116
thematic units, 121, 126
Scheduling. *See* Timetable
School administration
development of partnership, 60
role in resource center, 4–5
support for resource center program, 24
teacher-librarians and, 8
School librarian. *See* Teacher-librarians
School libraries, contemporary, 2
School library resource center
available resources, 6–7
book exchanges and, 61–63
celebrations and, 82–84
collection location in, 11
concepts of program, 3–4
development of, 5fig.
displays and, 61, 63–64
education technology and, 13–14
evolution of, 2
human and community resources and, 67–68
nonprint materials, 65–66
physical environment of, 4
reading, 79–81
text sets in, 65
theme materials in, 65
traditional/contemporary, 2
types of collections, 7
writing and, 77–79
School volunteers. *See also* Parent volunteers
as writing mentors, 77–78
for book fairs, 81
Science and language arts fairs, 83
Selection. *See* Collection management